VIKING MUSÉET PÅ BORG

V Å G A N

MELBU

LAUKVIKA

FISKEBØL

GIMSØYA

TROLLFJORDEN

VALBERG

HENNINGSVÆR

KABELVÅG

SVOLVÆR

SKROVA

KEISERBESØK DIGERMULEN

DET ES

LOFOTAKVARIET

LOFOT- MUSÉET i VÅGAN

D1331093

ÖSTERBERG-95

Title: Guide to the History of Lofoten
Chief Editor and co-author: Gro Røde, historian, Ramberg, Flakstad, Lofoten.
Additional contributors:
Finn Myrvang, lecturer, Head of the Placename Project, Bø i Vesterålen.
Håkon Brun, teacher, Kabelvåg, Vågan.
Åsa Elstad, historian, Fellow of the University of Tromsø, Tromsø.
Håkon Glørstad, archaeologist, Oslo.
Zanette Tsigaridas, postgraduate student of archaeology, Oslo.
Marit Lund Horseide, Chief Officer of Culture and Leisure Services, Flakstad Municipal Council.
Ottar Schiøtz, Head of the Norwegian Fishing Village Museum, Å and Lofoten Tourist Enterprises AS (Ltd), Sørvågen, Moskenes.
Dag Sørli, Mayor, teacher and manager of Lofotboka publishers, Værøy.
Hans Arne Hansen, teacher, Røst.

This project is the result of a joint effort between Lofotrådet (the Lofoten Regional Council), 8370 Leknes, and the public museums of Lofoten.
Project leaders Ottar Schiøtz and Tom Moltu (Head of the Lofoten Museum)
Design, layout and image scanning: DataDesign, Robert Walker, 8392 Sørvågen.
English Translation: Robert Walker, DataDesign.
Print: as Joh. Nordahls Trykkeri (Ltd.), Oslo
ISBN 82-993764-1-6

Cover illustration:
Old cargo vessels, or "jekts", in Bergen harbour. Section of a water colour signed F.S. (F. Sørvig), 1866. Bergen Maritime Museum.
The Lofoten Fishery was of great importance to the development of Northern Norway. Lübeck and other North German towns, together with Norwegian coastal towns like Bergen, were dependent on commodities from the north. Every summer, stockfish, salt fish and barrels of cod-liver oil and salted roes were loaded aboard the broad "jekts", whereupon the Northerners hoisted the great square sails and raced to Bergen. The illustration shows fully loaded Nordland jekts approaching Bergen harbour ready to be tugged up to the quay and unloaded. In return for the fish products, the Northerners bartered wares that were essential in order to meet the long winter: goods derived from corn and flour, groceries and liquor, lines and ropes, canvas and sailcloth, fishing tackle and gifts like dress material, and baking and sweets for the families waiting at home.

Guide
to the History of Lofoten

The Lofoten Public Museums
The Lofoten Regional Council

Editor-in-Chief: Gro Røde

Contents

Glossary

Danish seines:	fishing gear, a kind of small trawl
fish racks:	wooden racks on which the cod are hung out to dry during the winter
handline:	single fishing line with hook and sinker
Hålogaland:	the old Norwegian name for North Norway
jekt:	broad sailing vessel used for freight purposes along the coast of Norway
klipfish:	cod or saithe, split, salted and dried
landlord/publican:	(Here:) local merchant with a monopoly on the sale of liquor, c. 1770 – 1870
longlines:	long fishing line, set horizontally, to which shorter, baited lines are attached at regular intervals
Nordland-type boats:	different types of old, wooden sailing/rowing vessels used for fishing (see page 32)
rorbu:	shack/wooden lodgings where the fishermen stayed and worked, especially during the major seasonal fisheries. Often on stilts along the shore
squire:	Wealthy merchant and landowner, often called "King of the Headland", with a monopoly on all trade and the right to determine all prices, etc. in his fishing village. (c. 1830 – 1940)
stockfish:	fish, usually cod or saithe, that has been dried in the open air on fish racks.

FOREWORD

Welcome to a journey through the history of Lofoten! We hope this *Guide* will give you an appetite for the diverse history of this wonderful island realm. Perhaps it will also make it easier for you, the reader, to understand the Lofoten of today.

Choosing just a few chapters from the history of Lofoten proved a difficult task, but we hope you will enjoy the result, and that it will give you a taste for more. The Guide is designed to help you travel from island to island – following local geography, as opposed to chronology. Among the main chapters you will also find smaller passages about anything from Stone Age settlements to the history of art in Lofoten.

The introductory chapter focuses on the reasons for human settlement in Lofoten – where fishing universally plays the role of common denominator. Each island has been given its own chapter, for the most part in connection with the various local public museums. In this way, you are not

only reading history, but are also given the opportunity of *experiencing* it. We recommend that you visit each island and each museum.

With your Guide in your hand, your journey can begin:
We start in the borough of Vågan, with the mediaeval town of Vågar. Mighty men lived here, and it was here that Norway's commercial fisheries were nurtured.

On the neighbouring island of Vestvågøy, we go back a few hundred years in time to the Iron Age and the Chieftain's Homestead at Borg. Here, we are given an insight into how great a centre of power scientists believe that this homestead was, socially, economically, politically and religiously.

Remaining on the same island, we move westward to Vestvågøy Museum in the old schoolhouse at Fygle, built towards the end of the 1800's. Here, you will find an interesting presentation of school and administrative history. The fisherman-farmer homestead in Skaftnes is also part of the Vestvågøy Museum – and a sub-chapter provides an account of everyday life on such a farm.

Proceeding across the Nappstraumen Strait, we arrive in Flakstad, ready for a visit to the Fisheries Museum in Sund. Here you will hear the drone of boat engines. The main theme here is the motorisation of the fishing fleet, and the consequences this had on people and communities. In Moskenes we visit the Norwegian Fishing Village Museum in Å. This chapter provides a short account of life in a small fishing village at the turn of the century.

We continue across the Maelstrom and land on the island of Værøy. There are no museums to visit here, but on the other hand, there is the tiny, abandoned hamlet of Måstad. Here, optimal use was made of all available natural resources; that is, until "progress" reached this place, too.

Our journey ends at the farthest island outpost – in Røst. Here, we read about the Italian nobleman, Querini – shipwrecked in 1432 – and about a contemporary folk culture whose roots are found in the ability to harvest what nature had to offer, of both birds and fish.

Find your own favourite island – and your own period of history, but do get acquainted with the rest of the island realm, too.

Travel, read and learn!

Gro Røde
Editor

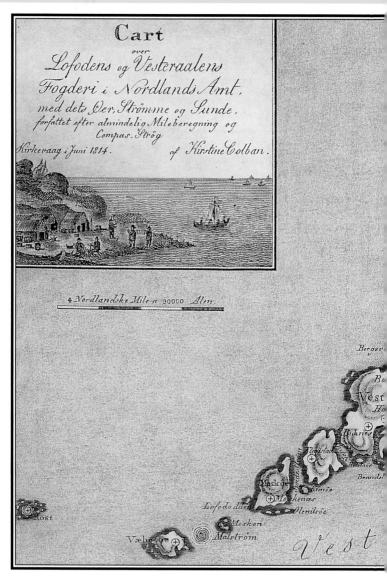

Map of Lofoten.

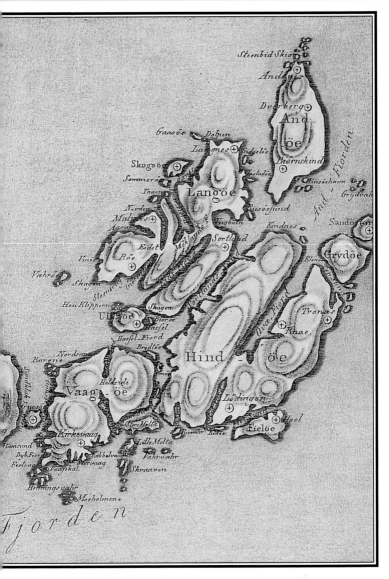

Drawn by Kirstine Colban – Kirkevåg in June, 1814

The Lofoten Islands

Like Pearls on a String

From east to west, the islands of the Lofoten archipelago stretch out like pearls on a string: Austvågøy, Gimsøy, Vestvågøy, Flakstadøy and Moskenesøy. Værøy and Røst are the farthest out to sea, separated from the other islands by the fabled Maelstrom – Moskstraumen. When travelling to the other islands, the people of Værøy and Røst say that they are "going to Lofoten", but even so, they still regard themselves as thoroughbred Lofoteners. They share the same geography, yet the islands are different in how the weather effects them, in how the people live, and in the natural resources harvested there. Thus the islands can offer exciting variations in both nature, culture and history.

The "Outer Coast" and the "Inner Coast"

Geographically, we often distinguish between the "inner coast" and the "outer coast" of Lofoten. The outer coast faces the Norwegian Sea and the inner coast faces the Vestfjord, and is where most of the settlement can be found. The outer coast is more exposed to the heavy, wet sea mists and fog, and the fierce and raging storms. This is was probably what inspired district governor G.P. Blom to write the following in 1827:

"*As ugly as the eastern coast of Lofoten is, it is yet surpassed in sheer rawness by the western coast, where, moreover, the fierce northerly and north-westerly storms rage with a greater vehemence than on the east coast, which is protected by the tall mountains.*"

The inner coast is characterised by calmer weather and rather warmer summer temperatures. Furthermore, the people there are spared from the horrid "good weather fog" that can come rolling in from the sea after a few warm, summer days. The sea fog covers the houses on the outer coast like a blanket, and temperatures drop instantly. In such cases we are glad that the inner coast is not too far away, because the sun may well be shining there, even from a cloudless sky. However, the outer coast does have its advantages, too. It is there that the land-scape can be bathed in the Midnight Sun between about May 25 and July 17. And in

From the harbour in Stamsund. The Skjærbrygga warehouse at centre. Fishing boats and cargo vessels, sloops, all in a row. (Photo: Annie Giæver c. 1900. Tromsø Museum.)

August, the sun may be even more beautiful – setting in a pale violet sea, and leaving the sky in shades of colour that no painter can ever hope to imitate.

Primeval Mountains and Barren, Rocky Ground

Lofoten is comprised of the youngest and the oldest types of rock we know. The latter are so-called primeval rocks and are among the oldest in the world, being the remnants of a once enormous 3 billion year old plateau. The island of Moskenesøy is the only one of the Lofotens that can boast of being composed in part of this oldest, primeval ground. From the shore, these mountains tower up, steep and sheer, towards the sky. On top, however, they become gentle, undulating, and flat. The "younger" mountains have sharp peaks, sharp ridges and are often referred to as an "alpine landscape". The mountains of Lofoten are so high that scientists believe they were not covered by ice during the last Ice Age which took place about 18,000 – 20,000 years ago. But bear with us, Lofoten is more than just mountains and rocks.

Combined Fishing and Farming

The islands of Austvågøy and Gimsøy have relatively good agricultural potential along their outer coasts, but these areas are, however, small in comparison to those on the island of Vestvågøy, in the middle of Lofoten. This island comprises one of the most important agricultural areas in the county of Nordland. In the middle of the island there are wide, flat fields and many farms surrounded by high, protecting mountains. Sub-zero temperatures can be rather more discernible here in this "inland" region than out in the villages by the sea.

Further to the west you will find the islands of Flakstadøy and Moskenesøy. There is less soil here, and farms become scarcer and smaller the further west you go. The islands seem to consist mainly of mountains and rocks. On the narrow expanse of coastline between the precipitous mountains and the open sea, settlers have bravely dug in. Having said this, the farming hamlets on the outer coast of Flakstad are luxuriant in comparison to Moskenes. The borough of Moskenes languishes in last place in the table of agricultural statistics. And as we continue further out to Værøy and Røst, the typical Lofoten pattern appears even clearer:

"Man on board, wife on land"

Out here, fish has always been the most important commodity, but way into this century the families of Lofoten were also dependent on having small farms, and on utilising what resources the land had to offer. In the

Him on board, her at home. They met at the landing place. (Photo: Bernt Sønvisen, 1995)

Summer meant haymaking at Hell, on the now abandoned outer coast of Moskenesøy island, 1937. (Norwegian Fishing Village Museum, Å)

mountain realm of Lofoten, even the landless classes could keep domestic animals by making use of the green and fertile, yet almost inaccessible mountainside hayfields. The local inhabitants climbed high up on the mountainsides to harvest fodder for their cows and sheep. Life was based on good fishing in combination with the keeping of domestic animals and the running of a *small* farm.

The women were for the most part responsible for the home , the farm and the domestic animals. They took care of what we call subsistence economy, providing important income that is not revealed in any tax assessments or documents. The men took care

of fishing, ensuring a flow of cash income to pay taxes and buy essential goods like flour, firewood, paraffin, sugar and tackle.

Throughout the 1960's and 70's this type of combined fishing and farming died out and the small farms gradually disappeared. The men became full-time fishermen all-year-round, or got other jobs, and women began to seek employment outside the home.

Today, only a few families stick to the traditional combination of fishing and farming, but the small farm buildings still remain a typical part of the Lofoten landscape. Moreover, it would seem that a number of younger families are to some extent bringing back the traditional combination of fishing and farming. In the 1990's, the local authorities on the island of Røst, encourage people to keep sheep – and they are in fact succeeding. In 1994, lamb from Lofoten was voted the best in the world, perhaps this too has encouraged others to start keeping sheep?

Shepherding on Mount Storfjellet, Røst, early summer, 1957.
(Hans A. Hansen)

Transport – Past and Present

"What would we do without the sea – carry our boats?"
This humorous remark is really not too far fetched, at least not in Lofoten. On the archipelago a boat means everything. Indeed, only a few decades ago, there were no roads in Lofoten. The Lofoten Road starts at Fiskebøl in the borough of Vågan and ends up on the island of Moskenesøy, at the fishing village of Å. The road out here is one long, narrow cultural monument. It meanders ever westwards, digging in on even the steepest cliff faces of the Hamnøy mountains, penetrating even the most porous parts of the Rørvik range. As late as in 1963, the final stage of the road was opened by the late King Olav V, who thereby made his own contribution to the history of communications in western Lofoten. Only a few years ago, there were ferry links between the Lofoten Islands. Now, bridges have been built over the straits and fjords. In 1989, the tunnel between Vestvågøy and Flakstad was opened. The only remaining ferry within the region works the crossing between Svolvær and Digermulen in the eastern part of Vågan, and the island of Skrova. Apart from that, we only catch ferries to and from Lofoten. To get to our island realm, you have to cross the sea – either by boat or by air. Lofoten's road link with the mainland – Lofast – will be the next project.

"The Four Flows"

Lofoten protrudes from the mainland and into the sea like an outstretched arm. The location of the islands catches the eye, and they are therefore displayed on many old and ancient maps. Such an arm-like position catches indeed most things, particularly gale force winds, storms and rain ..., but the most important thing this arm embraces is the invisible, life-giving **Gulf Stream**. The Gulf Stream strokes intimately past the Lofoten Islands, creating mild winters, both at sea and on land. Without the Gulf Stream, Lofoten, with its northerly location, would become a cold and desolate place. It would be too cold for people to live on the islands, the **Norwegian Arctic cod** would not follow the flow to the archipelago, **visiting fishermen** would not come from north and south, and the thousand-year-old flow of **fish products** to the world beyond could never have happened.

Tradition of Openness

Lofoten – an all-embracing arm, an inverted fjord? There is a long-standing tradition of openness here, openness when receiving visitors, openness towards news from afar. Experienced genealogists say that old censuses from Lofoten make exciting reading because, over the past couple of hundred years, such a surprisingly large amount of the population has moved here from other regions. People came here from the north and the south, from fjords and valleys – and also from other countries. Lofoten has received visiting fishermen, artists, peddlers and adventurers – and Lofoteners have set out on journeys, too, taking their fish with them. All this has provided new contacts and new impulses. For the most part, all this activity and flow of people was typical of the winter months. Today, the major flow of visitors comes during the summer season, constituting a relatively new and exciting chapter in the history of Lofoten. The main activity, however, still takes place during the winter, when the cod arrive.

The Amazing Journey of the Cod

Lofoten's be all or end all is inextricably linked to the world's greatest cod harvest, which takes

The four flows that "created" Lofoten – The Gulf Stream from the south, the cod from the north, boats and fishermen from north and south and the flow of fish products out to world markets. (Illustration: Liv Østerberg, 1995)

place from January to April. The Vestfjord, between the islands and the mainland, has been called the world's biggest maternity ward. It is here the Norwegian Arctic cod come to spawn during the winter. Until the age of 7 or 8, they frolic in the Barents Sea before reaching sexual maturity, whereupon they set off on a most amazing journey back to their place of birth. The journey begins in November-December. The cod steal past Finnmark and Troms, some of them being caught here and there, finally reaching Lofoten in enormous numbers in January, after a journey of some 800 kilometres.

Lofoten Draws Them

Why do the cod migrate to the same area every year? Perhaps we might say that the cod has a kind of "instinct" leading it to its goal? Scientists say that this is still one of Nature's mysteries, but they do know that a number of favourable conditions in Lofoten attract the cod: Perfect spawning temperatures of 4-6 degrees in the sea, correct salinity, suitable depth, appropriate currents and sufficient sustenance for the offspring (crawfish larvae and red copepod larvae). A 5 kilo female cod lays 2.5 million eggs, of which about 20 survive and develop into fish during the first

The catch is landed, gutted, tied and hung up on the shore. The year is c. 1917. (Photo: Wilse. Norwegian Folk Museum's photo collection)

year. Despite such great losses, the future of the species is thus safeguarded, and it is left to man to harvest the seas in a responsible and sustainable manner.

Poet and clergyman, Petter Dass, expressed Nordland's dependency on the fisheries. His words were written in the 1690's, and they still apply:

"Yea! The fish in the seas are our daily bread,

Should we lose them, we will suffer and dread,

Forced to utter our miserable sighs."

The Lofoten Aquarium

The Lofoten Aquarium was established by the Kabelvåg Fisheries Company in 1931. By 1985, the old aquarium had suffered so much wear and tear that it had to be closed down. In 1989, however, a new aquarium was to be found in its proper element – with the sea rippling around its quayside columns. The main objective of the aquarium is to show what is to be found in the seas of Lofoten, from the shore to the deep. Here, visitors are received by seals that clap their flippers and bark hoarsely ; here you can stand face to face with a wolf fish, or a cod if you like; or you can study the great claws of the spider crab. Life in the seas can provide a wealth of exciting discoveries.

Sakrisøy: *The wild mountains and narrow shoreline did not stop people from settling in Lofoten. A small, natural harbour, like the one here in Sakrisøy, was often enough to gain access to the abundant fish resources in the Vestfjord. (Photo: Ottar Schiøtz)*

Gunnar Berg: The Battle of Troldfjord. *Dramatic meeting between old and new: On March 6, 1890, rich boat owners closed off the Troldfjord, which was teeming with fish, with the help of steamships.*

The fishermen, in their open, Nordland-type boats were prevented from fishing freely in the fjord. After many hours of strife, they broke the barricade and fishing could continue in the traditional manner.

Ballstad, old rorbu cabin *(Gulbrandsen)*
Ballstad, a traditional, active fishing village overlooking the Vestfjord.
For a thousand years, visiting fishermen from all along the coast have
had the fishing villages of Lofoten as their base during the winter fishing

season. Many had to spend the night under their sails, under their over-
turned vessels, under rocks or in caves. Gradually, rorbu cabins were
built; small, timber buildings where the fishermen could live and work
during the Lofoten fishing season.

Arable land at Unstad on the island of Vestvågøy *(Photo: Vebjørn Storeide)*
In order to survive in the north, the Northerners had to combine a number
of different activities: fishing, fish processing, hunting and agriculture –

and over the past decades, also construction work, carpentry and tourism – each to its own season. Even in Vestvågøy, one of North Norway's major farming communities, it was normal to have more than one job.

The Fisherman and the Cod: *The days of the small open boats are over. Even so, the fishermen still often take smaller boats out to catch cod for drying, salting, filleting or just to boil fresh together with liver and roes. They call the latter variety "mølje", and it is a delicacy here in Lofoten. (Photo: Ottar Schiøtz)*

The Lofoten Fishery

We wait for them, the fish and the fishermen, in January, every single year. Irrespective of occupation or business, in Lofoten, everyone is preoccupied with the winter fishery; with how things are going. This male-dominated occupation is observed with Argus-eyed vigilance by housewives, furniture salesmen, teachers and tax officers. They all know that the greatest cod fishery in the world, forms the basis of all human settlement in the Lofotens.

At sea in Vågan. (Photo: Wilse. Norwegian Folk Museum photo collection)

Thousand Year Tradition

From January to April the fishermen are always at their posts in Lofoten, ready and waiting. In about 1120, King Øystein built "rorbu" cabins in Lofoten, where the fishermen could live and work. This was almost certainly because of the many visiting fishermen that came to the fishing villages during the Winter Season. Consequently, even more came.

In such a way, the total catch increased, and the King gained greater income and more control over the wealth that was landed. Today, the fishermen, and this "commercial fishery", are thus integral parts of a thousand year old tradition. The fishermen do as their forefathers did, they catch tasty cod, full of fatty liver and nutritious roes.

The fish as a commodity is the same, the drying method is the same, but apart from this the methods used for fishing, production and sales have all changed.

Stone Age finds show that the people here harvested the seas using tackle like stone sinkers and hooks made of horn and bone. Nets were also used, but only in shallow waters. The deep sea haul was taken with hook and line – handlines. This continued for thousands of years, until way into the Middle Ages. In the history of the Lofoten Fishery, the tackle in use has been the focus of much turbulence. Being innovative on the seas of Lofoten has been no easy task. The fishermen were traditionally very sceptical to the use of new types of gear, saying that "the old ones are good enough". But more important was probably the fear of having to make new, substantial investments in an uncertain trade. Most of them had enough debt to begin with ...

Turbulence and Prohibition

We know that longlines were used in the Vestfjord in 1533, but it was not until 1580 that they became commonplace. The handliners quickly became frustrated, complaining that longlines ruined the fishing for them. There were no regulations on fishing, and lawlessness reigned: no rules for when the day's fishing should begin, and no rules determining what tackle could be used. No wonder people were in despair. They asked the King for help, and were heard. In 1644, King Christian IV banned longlining. Gillnets were introduced to cod fishing in about 1750, and there was no lack of protest at that either. Consequently, nets were banned for a brief period of time. Only handlines were to be used, but then there were new protests, and the ban had to be lifted.

Indeed, neither making laws nor buying tackle were easy matters – you never knew what would be prohibited next winter. Should the winter season prove to be a bad one, then the new types of tackle were held to blame, and there was a great deal of confrontation in the fishing villages between handliners, longliners and gillnetters. Things went to and fro, bans were imposed and the same bans were lifted. In the 1770's, both gillnets and the illegal longlines were in use. In 1786, both types of tackle were finally made legal, but conditions in the fishing villages were still a

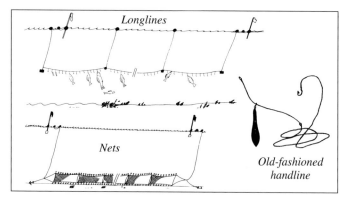

Longlines

Nets

Old-fashioned handline

cause of great concern, with large numbers of strangers, few regulations, and a disturbingly high consumption of liquor and luxury commodities.

The Lofoten Act –Improved Order at Sea

In 1816, the Lofoten Act – *Lofotloven* – was passed. This act regulated the time when fishing could begin in the morning, and divided the seas off the shore of each fishing village into permanent areas for longlining and gillnetting. The landlords or publicans of each fishing village were made inspectors, making sure that everyone conformed to the new regulations. So now peace was finally supposed to reign in the fishing villages, since the fishermen were obliged to stick to their own fishing village, rent "rorbu" cabins there, and decide in advance what type of tackle they would be using. There was, however, great dissatisfaction with these arrangements. The law was too rigid, it was not adapted to the unpredictable ways of the fishery. The fish did not distribute themselves evenly among the fishing villages, sometimes they were here, sometimes there.

Being bound to one part of Lofoten where there were no fish was quite intolerable when people in other areas were hauling in the catch. Furthermore, the landlords, having attained considerable authority, had become landowners – like the British squires – and acted like minor sheriffs in each individual fishing village, running things as they pleased. Dissatisfaction was rife, both among the fishermen, the general public, and among the official class.

Free Waters – Free Fishing

In 1857 the strict regulations were finally lifted. An important figure in the implementation of this was government official Ketil Motzfeldt. The basic principles for fishing now became: free waters, free fishing, state inspection. The landlords, or squires, were removed from their office as inspectors, and the fishermen were given more influence and freedom – at least on paper. In reality, many fishermen were still tied to their fishing villages. The squires had lent them money to outfit their boats, and had allowed them credit when times were hard. The squires knew that the fishermen would be forced to turn to them, even though they offered poor prices for their fish. Those who were in debt had simply no choice. The freedom to set tackle wherever the fishermen pleased led once again to unrest and disturbance. Nets and longlines were often set too close, and were ruined.

Safety and Minimum Prices

With the advent of the motor boat, work at sea became both easier and safer. It was easier to follow the fish and it was easier to go where the best prices were paid. The year 1938 is very important in the history of the Norwegian fisheries: it was then that the Raw Fish Act came into force, ensuring the fishermen a fixed price for their fish. From now on, the fish buyers could no longer determine the value of the catch, this was left instead to the fishermen's own organisation, the Raw Fish Sales Association. The fishermen were secured a minimum price and could once again hold their heads high.

Up until the Second World War, fish caught in Lofoten was either sold to the squire, or to buyer boats anchored up in the harbour. After the war, the buyer boats disappeared, but even so, the squires were no longer the only buyers – others had appeared on the scene. The 1950's and 60's were tough times for the old, well-established squire-owned businesses; they went bankrupt, one after the other. For the fishing village communities, this transition meant uncertain times – but also opened up new opportunities.

The Seas of Lofoten Today

Today, the seas of Lofoten are divided up into longline, gillnet and Danish seine areas during the winter fishery and it is the fishermen themselves who determine the divisions. The boats must remain strictly in their own areas. The handliners on the other hand, can fish wherever they please. Nets and longlines catch the most fish, but the handliners dominate in numbers. However, according to the fisheries inspectorate in Svolvær, the tendency is clear: Danish seiners are increasing year by year. The Danish seiners use a small trawl net, like a large sack, that is tightened around the fish. Many fishermen criticise the Danish seine, saying that it is worse for the fish resources than the purse seines that purged the seas in the 1950's, before they were banned. Unrest and animosity between the users of the various types of fishing gear still oc-

Out on the fishing grounds. From the Lofoten Fishery, 1939. (Photo: The Coast Guard. Vestvågøy municipal photo collection.)

cur, and the fishery inspectors of Lofoten have to patrol the waters off Lofoten throughout the season, to make sure that the borders between the different types of gear are observed.

Crisis and Optimism

Towards the end of the 1980's, some local communities experienced a crisis after the Lofoten fishery had provided poor yields for a number of consecutive years. During the winter of 1995, however, things were once again looking up – the number of fishermen taking part was on the increase and the total catch was once again at an acceptable level. The fish kept to the more distant banks, though, and those who made money were the larger gillnetters and Danish seiners. The winter fishery was a disappointment for the smaller handliners, both in volume and income.

The Lofoten Fishery is culture and craftsmanship based on strong, long-standing and proud traditions. The Lofoten Fishery is competitiveness coupled with team work. It is long working days and worn out workers. It is hours spent at the most exhilarating, most dangerous and most beautiful place of work imaginable. It is elation at a major haul and sorrow over losses, purged seas and the fight for resources.

Table showing participation and total quantity of fish caught during the Lofoten Fishery. A few selected years.
(Note that until 1929, the catch was counted, not weighed)

Year	No. of men	No. of fish (in 1000's)	(tons)
1885	26.652	26.500	86.400
1895	32.600	38.600	123.520
1904	18.000	12.290	39.328
1913	14.659	10.200	32.640
1921	17.095	18.600	59.520
1928	25.216	34.000	108.800

Year	No. of men	(tons)
1929	27.054	130.256
1933	31.905	80.695
1939	25.803	115.318
1945	16.150	67.716
1947	20.533	145.897
1959	9.819	44.177
1966	4.508	24.438
1978	4.882	57.441
1987	2.616	17.897
1995	4.678	50.517

The Nordland-type boat
- a sailing sculpture

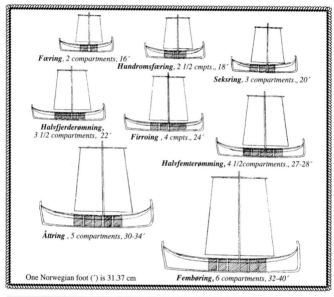

Færing, 2 compartments, 16´

Hundromsfæring, 2 1/2 cmpts., 18´

Seksring, 3 compartments., 20´

Halvfjerderømning, 3 1/2 compartments, 22´

Firroing, 4 cmpts., 24´

Halvfemterømning, 4 1/2 compartments., 27-28´

Åttring, 5 compartments, 30-34´

One Norwegian foot (´) is 31.37 cm

Fembøring, 6 compartments, 32-40´

Hardly any other type of Norwegian boat has been described in more detail and more often than the Nordland-type boats. Today, they have become more or less accepted as the very symbol of this part of the country. Many an artist has been inspired by their picturesque appearance, and their contours that bring the Viking ships to mind. Geographically, no other type of boat has been so widespread as these, from the River Namsen in northern Trøndelag, to the Kola peninsula in Russia. These boats more or less monopolised the Lofoten fishery, from the smallest "færing" to the largest "åttring" and "fembøring". Nordland-type boats are renowned for being good rowing and sailing boats. While they were still being used for fishing, they were mythicised by the fishermen themselves. They had an eye for these boats and could quickly assess their quality. It is said that they took great delight in telling stories about boats and the weather, about sailing, and about great feats at sea in competition with each other. Boat owners had status, the bigger the boat, the better. Grandest was the status of the captain, or *høvedsmann*, on board the larger Nordland-type boats.

The Cod Liver Oil Factory

Down by the old harbour, near the beach where they used to haul up the boats, you will find the oldest production plant in Å, the cod-liver oil factory. Here, the fish were braced and hung up on the fish racks to dry, or they were split and salted to make klipfish. The roes were salted in enormous German wine vats of oak, and the cod liver was boiled or steamed into cod liver oil.

In the old days, the liver was just left in the vats and the cod liver oil was skimmed off as the liver fermented in the heat of summer. Later, they began to boil the cod liver in iron cauldrons in order to extract a greater yield of valuable cod liver oil. This was done all year round. The stench was rife all over the fishing village. "You can smell money," people said of both this and the smell of dried fish.

The old Norse name for cod liver oil was "lysi" – light, and the oil was actually used to fuel lamps all over Europe. Moreover, it was used for tanning skins, in the manufacture of paint and soap, and lots more. Cod liver oil and stockfish were for centuries Norway's most valuable commodity.

Every summer, thousands of barrels of cod liver oil were transported on cargo vessels, the so-called "jekt"s, from Lofoten to Bergen and further on to Europe.

Fish, liver and roes, cooked together and referred to as "mølje", have always been an important and healthy part of the coastal people's diet. Vitamins A and D and the Omega 3 unsaturated fatty acids in the cod liver oil, helped keep people healthy. It was often said that the cod liver oil makers and other people that took a lot of cod liver oil were seemingly never ill.

Medicinal Cod Liver Oil

Pharmacist Peter Møller wanted to introduce more people to the healthy effects of cod liver oil. In 1854, he built a lined cauldron, filled the space between the cauldron and its lining with water, and steam-boiled the fresh cod livers. In this way he greatly improved the quality of the oil. The invention of medicinal cod liver oil was honoured with awards at many trade fairs in Norway and abroad. Later, the cod liver was steamed in conical oak barrels. In order to extract the last remaining drops of precious cod liver oil, the residue of the liver was then squeezed in a liver press before going to the manufacture of cattle feed or fertiliser.

Today, much of the old production equipment can still be seen in the cod liver oil factory at the Norwegian Fishing Village Museum in Å. Cod liver oil is still produced there in the old fashioned manner, and small bottles of it together with cod liver oil lamps are on sale as mementoes from Lofoten.

Røst 1990 - 1150 hectoliters of cod-liver oil were produced. (Photo: Helge A. Wold)

The Sea Gives, The Sea Takes Away ...

The sea is a fickle and dangerous place of work. Almost every winter, someone was "left behind" at sea. Many men met a watery grave, and in Lofoten you will find several common grave stones and monuments dedicated to tragic losses at sea. It was when the fishing was done in large open rowing boats that the major disasters occurred.

February 11, 1849: The Lofoten fleet was out on the fishing grounds when the weather suddenly changed. A north-westerly storm with hurricane force winds wiped the seas clean. Five hundred men were lost on that day. Thousands of people lost a husband, a father, a son, a brother, a friend.

And there were other years, too: On March 31, 1868, 100 men were drowned in a storm. In 1893, 119 were lost at sea in Lofoten and Vesterålen. And here in Lofoten we remember March 30, 1946. The 52 foot fishing boat "Brattegg" was smashed to smithereens just off the breakwater in Laukvik, on the outer coast of the island of Austvågøy. 14 men were on their way home with their share of the profits after the season was over. Not one of them made it. The oldest was 47, the two youngest were just 17.

In Lofoten today, more people are killed in traffic accidents than at sea. But when drowningsdo occur, they have a devastating effect on the local communities, the people have traditionally learned to fear such accidents.

Despite new technology, colour echo sounders, navigational systems and satellite navigators, a safe, traditional type of insurance is found in the companion boat. The boats compete over the catch, yet they wait for each other, approaching and leaving the fishing grounds together. Technology is not always enough – the sea and the weather cannot be tamed!

"They didn't come home." In remembrance of those lost on the "Brattegg". (Photo: Helge Wold.)

S

STOCKFISH

Lofoten is one of the best places in the world for producing stockfish. The further west you go in Lofoten, the better – in Værøy and Røst, conditions are particularly favourable. Visiting the Lofoten Islands in May is an experience for both the nose and the eyes, when knolls and hilltops are covered with fully laden stockfish racks. The island residents open their arms and proudly declare, "That's our money you see hanging there."

Pure Food – No Additives

No other country can compete with this way of conserving good food. Many have tried, none have been too successful – like Iceland, for instance, who completed their final trial year in 1992. The fact is that very strict demands are made on conditions in stockfish production areas:
The air must not be too dry and the temperature must be relatively low so that the fish is not ruined by maggots and flies. On the other hand, the air must be warm enough so as to avoid freezing. A continuous breath of wind, with a touch of seaborne salinity, provides the best results.

Stockfish is a healthy, fresh commodity chemically free from artificial additives, created almost from "fresh air and love" alone. The production process is resource friendly and beyond all doubt the least energy-demanding food manufacturing procedure in the world. All the nutrition of fresh fish remains in the dried fish, only the water is removed. The nutritional value of a kilo of stockfish is the equivalent of that of 5 kilos of fresh fish.

Under reasonable storage conditions, stockfish will keep for years. When immersed in water, it soaks up all the moisture again, and in terms of transport economics it is therefore a unique foodstuff for export purposes.
Indeed, stockfish was in fact one of the first foodstuffs from the animal kingdom to be the object of international trade.

"Prima", "Sekunda" and Africa

Normally, the stockfish is taken down from the fish racks in early June and traditionally, June 12 was "fish-fetching day". From then on, it is the fish grader's turn to sort the fish in accordance with the various different criteria. It is said that the stockfish grader not only does his job, but that he is also a craftsman in his field: he must be able to quickly see, smell and assess. At first, the fish is roughly sorted into 3 main categories: 1) "Prima" – or first class, 2) "Sekunda" – or second class, and 3) Africa (tertiary). Subsequently, it is sorted into a whole host of varieties, up to 30, according to quality, thickness and length.

The origins of this system lead us back to the time of the Hanseats (and later that of the merchants of Bergen) and their ability to exploit the demands made by the various markets on taste and size. Stockfish bound for Italy is graded with particular accuracy. There are at least 12 different grades of "first class" Lofoten

cod. In addition, there are at least 5 different types of "second class" cod. "First class" cod from Lofoten is sorted by length, weight and appearance, into the various classes shown in the table below.

First and second class cod from Finnmark is sorted by weight – 100/200, 200/400, 400/600, 600/800 and 1000/1200 grams per fish.

Most stockfish is exported, something which is reflected in the names of the different categories. In the 1300's, the export of stockfish constituted no less than 80% of Norwegian export income. In 1994, 4824 tons of stockfish were exported at a value of NOK 392 millions. There are 30 countries on the list of buyers of this exalted commodity. At the

Sorting categories – First Class Lofoten Cod
- Ragno, 60 cm over
- WM, Westre Magro 50/60 (thin Westre), 50-60 cm
- WM, Westre Magro 60/80 (thin Westre), 60-80 cm
- WDM, Westre Demi Magro 60/80 (semi-thin Westre), 60-80 cm
- WDM, Westre Demi Magro 50/60 (semi-thin Westre), 50-60 cm
- GP, Grand Premiere, 60-80 cm
- WC, Westre Courant (ordinary Westre), 75-80 fish per 50 kg
- WP, Westre Piccolo (small Westre), 100-120 fish per 50 kg
- WA, Westre Ancona, 75-80 per 50 kg
- HO, Hollender (ordinary Dutch), 58-60 fish per 50 kg
- BR, Bremer, 50-55 fish per 50 kg
- Lub, 40-45 fish per 50 kg

Second class Lofoten cod is sorted into the following categories:
- IG, Italia Grande (large Italian) 55-60 fish per 50 kg
- IGM, Italia Grande Magro(large, thin Italian) 60-65 fish per 50 kg
- IM, Italia Medio (medium Italian) 75-80 fish per 50 kg
- IMM, Italia Medio Magro (medium thin Italian), over 80 fish per 50 kg
- IP, Italia Piccolo (small Italian) 100-120 fish per 50 kg
- IPP, Italia Piccolo Piccolo (small, thin Italian) over 120 per 50 kg

top of the list, Italy prevails un-challenged, importing 3946 tons. It is therefore not without good reason that the Mayor of Røst says, "God bless Italian house-wives and their kitchens! Long live Italian cuisine!" In 1994, other important buyers included Croatia, the USA, Great Britain, Nigeria, France and Germany.

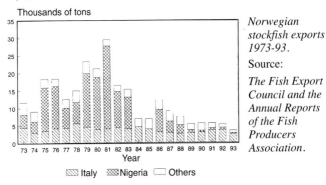

Thousands of tons

Year

Italy Nigeria Others

Norwegian stockfish exports 1973-93.
Source:
The Fish Export Council and the Annual Reports of the Fish Producers Association.

– Stockfish Grading in the Year 1750 –

Stockfish is divided into two main groups, round fish and split fish. Round fish has been gutted – i.e. the stomach has been slit and the innards and head removed. The fish are coupled together two by two with string tied around the tails, and are hung up like that to dry. Split fish is fish that has been decapitated and split along the belly and backbone, leaving it connected only at the tail. In Lofoten today, round fish is totally predominant.

The grading of stockfish is an old art dating back to the times when the Hanseats and the Dutch had control of stockfish trade in Bergen. Written sources from 1750 show that split stockfish was also sorted into many different classes.

Rotskjær Herrenfisk, Lübsk Zartfisk, Stor Zartfisk, Hollender Zartfisk,
Dansk Zartfisk, Kehlvækker fisk, Lübsk Vækkerfisk, Hamburger Høkerfisk,
Dansk Høkerfisk, Lübsk Losfisk, Hamburger Losfisk
Middelfisk, Småfisk, Søndmør Rotskjær, Mager Rotskjær, Udskud Rotskjær,

In 1890, the multifarious sorting system was made simpler, and today's split stockfish categories were adopted: Zartfisk, Vekkerfisk, Høkerfisk and Danskfisk.

(From: Bottolfsen, Ø. "Lüb og undermåls italiener," Lofotboka 1984)

A Norwegian Speciality:

"Lutefisk" – Cod in Lye

Lutefisk á la Chef de Lofoten:

One kilo of stockfish provides 3 kilos of "lutefisk". Immerse the stockfish in plenty of cold water and leave to soak for 8 days, changing the water every day. Use round fish and remove the spine when the fish has been sufficiently soaked. In my opinion, whole, or round fish stays whiter than split-dried fish.

Make lye from 30 litres of boiling water and 3 dessert spoonfuls of caustic soda, or, 2 litres of birch ashes and 7 litres of boiling water.
Cool the lye and pour it over the fish. leave for about 24-36 hours according to how "loose" a consistency you require of the fish. The longer it soaks in lye, the "looser" it becomes.
Afterwards, leave the fish under cold, running water for 1-2 days.

How to prepare "lutefisk":

If you are expecting big eaters, allow one kilo of fish per person. Normally, 400-700 grams should be enough.

Boil plenty of water and add 1 large dessert spoonful of salt per litre. When the water boils, add the thoroughly rinsed pieces of fish. Remove the pan from the heat and allow the fish to simmer – not boil – for 10-15 minutes.

With "lutefisk", the Chef de Lofoten serves lightly salted bacon and diced onions together with pease pudding and, of course, boiled potatoes.

Another variation: Serve with pease pudding, melted bacon fat, white sauce, mustard and bacon.

(From: Storeide, Mareno – "Fra Lofotkokkens gryte. Orkana Forlag.)

Stockfish Dish from Nigeria
(for four persons)
Three medium size stockfish (30 cm)
12 fresh red peppers (chilli)
Two large onions
320 g of tomato purée
25 cc of vegetable oil
75 cc of water
Finely chop the onion and the peppers and mix with the tomato purée.
Fry in the palm oil for about 10 minutes while adding water and salt to taste. Cut the stockfish into 5-8 cm thick slices and soak for at least half an hour before adding to the rest of the dish. Boil for about 15 minutes.

(From the newspaper "Aftenposten", 18 May, 1995)

Ballstad, 1987:
Sacks of stockfish ready for export to the Italian market.
(Photo: Helge A. Wold.)

Squire and "King of the Headland"

Originally, the fishing villages belonged to the King, and the inhabitants were all tenants, irrespective of whether they were fishermen, rich merchants, or cargo-ship owners. In the early 1800's, however, something rather unusual happened. The king was having financial difficulties and began selling his land in the fishing villages. Those who bought it, were the merchants, or the already established landlords/publicans in the fishing villages. In the course of a few decades, the fishing villages fell into private hands.

These new landowners, or "squires", settled in the fishing villages, by inlets or on the headlands, and were consequently also referred to as "nessekonger", meaning the "kings of the headlands".

The squires carried on a number of enterprises that had been going on since the old days, while at the same time keeping their eyes open for new and profitable ventures. New jobs were created and there was considerable activity in the fishing villages. The squire's most important contribu-

tion was probably first and foremost the organisation of trade based in the area where the fish were caught, as opposed to the earlier Bergen trade, where it was the merchants of Bergen who determined prices, sorting and exports. Freer trade, increased settlement and good fishing led to better times in the north. From then on, more of the income from trade in the north was invested in the north, and less in Bergen and northern Germany. Lofoten and North Norway experienced considerable financial growth.

"Out of the Frying Pan into the Fire?"

In the old fishing villages, before the advent of the system of landlords and squires, many people were to some extent dependent on the wealthy class of local merchants. Furthermore, we know that the northerners were in despair over the so-called "Nordland Debt" that was owed to the merchants of Bergen. The relationship between them was onesided; those who caught and supplied the fish always ended up in the red, but Bergen was a long way away, and control was difficult...

Some historians therefore maintain that for the fisherman and his family, relating to a local squire and merchant was like getting out of the frying pan only to fall into the fire. The local merchant, as opposed to those in Bergen, had plenty of opportunity to collect any outstanding debt from the fisherman and his family. In this way, it was probably better for them to owe money to a distant merchant in Bergen, than to the local squire.

The squires had a monopoly on *all* trade and industry, including the buying and selling of fish and all other goods. They were landowners, and rented out "rorbu" cabins and fish racks, and the land on which to erect them. The squires were so powerful, that the fishermen believed that the great, untameable ocean also belonged to them. Until the early 1900's, the fishermen were obliged to de-

Finnesset Trading Post near Kabelvåg. Watercolour by Kirstine Colban Aas (1811). Finnesset was licensed to serve alcoholic beverages in 1762, and was the first trading post in Northern Norway with royal privileges.
Kirstine Colban Aas (1791-1863) was a Lofoten lass and daughter of clergyman Erik Colban of Kabelvåg. She holds a central position in North Norwegian cultural history and in her own times she was well-known as a painter, author and North Norway's first literary critic.

(Original in Vågan Folkehøgskole. Photo: Thomas Røjmyr, Lofoten Museum.)

liver their catch to whomever they rented their "rorbu" cabins from. The fishermen and their families who were resident in the fishing villages were the squire's tenants, paying their rent with something in the region of 6 – 24 days of unpaid labour.

The atmosphere in the fishing villages was determined by the way the squire treated his tenants and their families. Some squires were caring and governed with common sense. They were often the ones to provide credit and surety so that the families were able to buy essential commodities and fishing tackle. Other squires abused their position and power, making life miserable for the villagers and depriving them of their freedom. The squire system's bane was the Raw Fish Act of 1936-38 which stripped the fish buyer and squire of the right to determine fish prices.

A State of Contemporary Lawlessness

You probably think all this must have happened a very long time ago? In 1939, there were 226 landed properties in the borough of Moskenes. 120 of them were owned by five local landowners. One of the these landowners was the local "king," owning an immense 71 properties. The local inhabitants constantly joined together and approached the authorities requesting that they inter-vene against the system of squires, or what they referred to as " a state of lawlessness." As late as in 1979, 100 "cotters" in one of the fishing villages asked for help in order to gain permission to buy the land on which their houses were built. This particular case was resolved, but even today, there are some fishing villages where remnants of the system of squires still remain.

Many people had a good relationship with the squire, as a human being, but gradually, the old *squire system* became the subject of strong criticism. It did not seem appropriate as ordinary people gained more and more political influence. *Democracy* was the objective, both locally and nationally. The system of squires, with its unilateral distribution of power and wealth, was now regarded as a prehistoric system, inconsistent with modern, political ideals.

*Portrait of the ageing
Kirstine Colban Aas*

Laburnum and Jasmine
– The Squire's Garden

In July the fields and roadsides are a sight for sore eyes. Wild flowers bloom in the most vivid and beautiful colours. Lowland flowers, mountain flowers and shoreline flowers grow side by side. Visitors are amazed by such luxuriance this far north, here at the "outer limits" of the Earth.

Gardening, however, is another matter. Cold summers could mean the end, both for flowers, and for their owner's patience. Today though, people keep at it, cultivating and nurturing their beautiful gardens, yet only a few decades ago, gardens were an upper class phenomenon.

The Hennum Garden, once belonging to Mrs. Kathrine Hennum of Å, was renowned for its beauty. A relative of hers describes it: "At the height of the summer it was at its most splendid, with hardwood trees like elm and laburnum; and the fragrance of bird cherry and jasmine. Around the cellar door there was a gateway of hops winding their way up the wall. Lupine, crocus, crown imperial, peony and lily, indeed, a whole host of flowers with foreign names could – with their fragrance and colours – stimulate the imagination with thoughts of far away places." The neighbouring garden was also beautiful. The squire's daughter, Ingrid Ellingsen, writes about her mother who worked in the garden: "During the spring and the summer she preferred to be down in the garden, working. She sowed seeds in forcing frames and planted flowers and vegetables. She obtained plants and perennials from the south, auriculas were among her favourites. In the vegetable garden she grew cauliflower, carrots, swedes, turnips, lettuce, parsley, radishes, sweet peas and beetroot."

Summer relaxation in Grandfather's garden in Å
(Central Office of Historic Monuments' photo archives.)

Traces of Sami Names in Lofoten

The Sami, or Lapps, were here, too. Old Lofoteners know this, and are not too surprised to find that Lappish place names are traceable here. On the island of Gimsøy you will find the crag called "Nilaberget", and round about you will find names like the Mærithaugen hill, deriving most likely from the Sami name of Máret. The name Mærit can also be found in conjunction with other local geographical phenomena like islets, slopes and headlands. In the borough of Vågan you will find the Saralapphellene and the Helsolia slope, in memory of the last reindeer Lapp in the area. The name Laborshaugen Hill, in the Buksnes district, probably derives from "lavuš", meaning small tent. The Ettemesdalen valley in Hol is just like a trough in the mountainside, but once there were probably lots of "ehtemas", a type of blueberry, there.

Many reminders of the Sea Sami

Sometimes, names have obvious Sami origins without having any reliable explanation: like the Algoelva river, the Algosletta field and the Algostranda beach on the island of Gimsøy, or the Ganggolandet beach in Hol, or Neiva, the spot in the Borge district where boats used to set out for the fishing grounds. But the word Pisselen, used of many small harbours in Røst as well as in Bisselvåg in Moskenes, reminds us of the lulesami word pissel meaning "to thrive, to have the patience to stay in one place" or "to be of such a nature that one remains in one place." The reason for this usage may refer to the actual landing place, the fishing, or to other factors. The island of Gjermesøya in the Buksnes district was known as Gjermarsøy in the 1400's. It is a tiny island, with a rather jagged shoreline and therefore probably provided shelter for many small vessels within a limited area. Consider the Sami word "gjerremas", which means spacious, profuse, or the word "gearpmaš" which means worm – although there are not many sand worms there. Perhaps the island itself is perceived as being "curled up" like a worm? The much discussed name of Kabelvåg may have been derived from "káble", meaning gable, a word also used to describe a headland. Consider "Andgavlen" = the Andøy gable or headland.

Natural Names Dominate

Gurratinden peak in the Hol district contains the syllable "gurra" which means crevice or crack, while Røssjelia and Skogbakkrøsjelia in the Borge district can be linked to the word "ružžu", which means deep, narrow pass.

Delp on the island of Gimsøy is a hamlet named after a mountain range: consider Delpen near Nyksund in Vesterålen, as well as the headland of Dealpo in Nesseby. The mountain island of Mosken near Værøy is inaccessible, consider the Sami word "moski," meaning "an inaccessible place." Perhaps the island was such an important landmark for seafarers that the entire Lofoten headland became known as Moskenes? In Mottolgrævan in Værøy there are frequent avalanches – consider the word "muohta", meaning snow, and "muohtalaš" meaning snowy. Perriken in Buksnes is a cleft, but referred, perhaps, originally to a peak, since the lulesami word "pærrak" means splinter. Innerraman and Ytterraman in Buksnes contain the syllable "rápma" meaning steep mountainside, wooded slope. Snevaggan in Moskenes probably consists of Norwegian "sne" - meaning slanting, and the Sami word "vággi" meaning a tiny valley by the sea.

Kjuklingdalen in Buksnes is easily compatible with the southern Sami word "tjuegkele" which means stony ground. Leknes might derive from "leahki" – low place, hollow, referring to the terrain near Leknessjøen. *Vadrian* in Buksnes are low hills and can be compared to the southern Sami "vaadare" which means gently rounded hills.

Kåkern, a sound with a bridge across it, probably has linguistic kinship with "goavki" which means rift or small opening. Mount Reka, the Rekdalen valley and the island of Rekøya/Rekøykeila probably have nothing to do with the old Norwegian word "reka" which is a kind of shovel. A more concrete meaning is provided by the Sami word "ráigi" which means "hole, opening, escape" as well as valley. Slupa and Eggumslupa in Borge are narrow, open inlets. It is here appropriate to compare the words with the lulesami word "sluhpú" which means narrow pass between a cliff and a river, or between two big rocks.

Joprim in Gimsøy is an area which was probably originally a bog. Compare then the Sami word "jobbirm" or "jobberm" meaning marshes or pond. Rebakmoa in Borge is near a marsh, compare with *ripák* meaning "muddy area, bog". The place name Buksnes, found on the islands of Vestvågøy and in Andøy, reminds us of the Sami word "buovča" – to be under water. Despite the lower sea level in more recent times, the high tide can still make the link feasible! The Refsholmen headland, Refsøya island, and inlets known as Refsvika in both Flakstad, Moskenes and Valberg, originate from the word "reakčá" which means "large, flat shore area with a clay bottom". Solkan in Hol is a mixture of Sami and Norwegian, "sulluk-an", the plural of "suolo" meaning islet. Svolvær, which until recently was written Suolvær, is Suolo-vearra, or the islet-village. Similarly we can consider the island of Soløya and the mountain of Solbjørn in Flakstad. The term Solvar used about the Breitind peak was derived from "Suolovárri", meaning islet-like mountain. Both the island of Vatterøya and the Vatterfjord in Vågan bring the southern Sami term "vaatere" to mind, meaning gnarl or wart when referring to rocky bumps.

We can be fooled by Norwegian explanations

This is just a selection of names that are, or might be, of Sami origin. In other cases we take for granted that names are Norwegian because they seem to be built up of solely Norwegian linguistic material. But some names with the apparently Norwegian prefix "Gull" (gold), for instance, may in fact come from "guolli" or "guelie" which means fish in Sami, or in other cases from "gullæ, golla" meaning "narrowing between two rocks". Innumerable names containing "Hund", which means dog in Norwegian, are merely derived from "unna-" meaning little or small. The syllable "kall" is probably derivative

of the Sami "gall-" which means rock, or cliff, and not necessarily of the Norwegian word for old-timer, "kall". Just as surprising is the fact that names containing "kjerring" do not necessarily derive from the Norwegian word "kjerring" meaning old woman: the Sami word "njuones-kærrek", meaning headland, is often perfectly applicable to landscapes where the Kjerring(nes) name appears, but the southern Sami word "gïerege" can also mean top, high end. A whole host of names containing "-kjerk" (resembling the Norwegian word for church) are not cultic memorials, but refer quite simply to the Sami word "kierké" or "gierkie" which means stone. Kjørrdalen comes from "čorru", meaning moraine, or stony ridge. Some names containing "Kobb-" have nothing to do with the animal (Norw-egian: seal), but with the Sami word "kobbo" which means rounded mound or hill, while names containing Kol-, often refer to long, low-lying places or depressions. The "Kors-" name very often derives from the Sami word "korsa" or "gorsa" meaning a small, deep crevice, or narrow valley. Names containing "lik" are not normally places where you find dead bodies (Norwegian: lik) or graves, but often reflect the Sami word "liige-" which means next to, or additional. Many names containing "Mørk-", particularly the Mørkdalen valley, contain the equivalent of the lulesami word "muorke", meaning strip of land between lakes, or headland, and has nothing to do with a lack of sunshine (Norwegian "mørk" = dark). Skutneset, Skutvika etc. sound Norwegian enough, but the Sami word "skuitu" is also applicable to such landscapes, whether they be "openings", "extensions" of lakes, marshes or fields, or simply narrow headlands. Slebrottet and Sleværet derive from the Sami word "slea∂∂u" meaning large, flat rock. "Spanna" used in reference to rocks and skerries etc. is the equivalent of southern Sami "spanjie" or "speanjoe" linked to a similar type of landmark. The name "Tjuv" (Norwegian for thief) occurs very often in place names, but refers seldom to criminals: the southern Sami words "tjuvve" and "tjovve" actually mean throat, but when it comes to place names, are used to denote an opening or mouth. Very many placenames containing "tjuv" are adjacent to, some kind of narrow opening or passage near the shore or on dry land.

Still a lot to learn ...

The reader must not be confused by the fact that many of these words have derived alternately from the northern Sami, Lulesami and Southern Sami languages, since many of the names originate from the distant past, when there were fewer differences in dialects than there are now.

Nordic languages, too, have grown apart, but it is nonetheless useful to compare Swedish and Danish or Icelandic and Faroese words with our own Norwegian words. Furthermore, we believe that both coastal Sami and reindeer Sami have left traces of their language behind in Lofoten's fjords and mountains, so the various Sami "traces" may originate from quite different periods and backgrounds.

Svolvær, which, way into historical times, was written Suolver (Suolo-verra) meaning island fishing village. Photo taken from Nonshaugen c. 1900 (Photo: F. Kramer. Lofoten Museum)

Vågan
– Big Brother in the East

The borough of Vågan is the welcoming gateway to Lofoten and consists of the southern part of the island of Austvågøy, together with the island of Gimsøy, a narrow strip of land on the island of Hinnøy, and several villages on smaller islands, including the important fishing villages of Henningsvær and Skrova. The name Vågan has an aura of history about it. There are archaeological excavations in Kabelvåg and Storvågan every summer, and many archaeological finds have also been made on the island of Gimsøy. The farming area known as Hov-Vinje was probably the homestead of the Vågan chieftain, Tore Hjort. A large rune stone dating back to the 900's was discovered on the Vinje farm on Gimsøy, and it can now be seen at the Tromsø Museum.

"The City"

Svolvær is the municipal centre of Vågan and "the city" of Lofoten. Here, the Lofoten Fisheries Inspectors have their headquarters, and the town also covers a number of administrative functions for the whole of Lofoten. Vågan is a large, traditional fisheries borough and is one of North Norway's major sea farming areas. The marine engineering industry is considerable, as is the case with other fisheries related services. Furthermore, the travel industry, commerce, and private and public services also provide a great many jobs.

Variety

The inhabitants of Vågan live in a variety of different villages and towns, the biggest of which are Svolvær and Kabelvåg. Kabelvåg is important from the viewpoint of cultural history, and the old wooden architecture there is of particular interest. In Henningsvær, the "Venice of the North", participants in the traditional fishing industry are rather sceptical of the major investments being made in tourism. Who will be able to buy fish when the landing stations have all been turned into galleries and hotels? There are a great number of contrasts in Vågan. Here, you will find everything from city life within an interweaving network of streets, to small, struggling hamlets in the Austre Vågan district with no road links whatsoever. There is variation in the natural surroundings, too: fjords, sharp mountain peaks, long beaches, gentle cloudberry marshes and flat agricultural areas.

The Lofoten Museum
– and The Vågan Trade Fair

The Lofoten Museum was established in 1976 and is Lofoten's regional museum. It is situated in Storvågan, just west of Kabelvåg, and has been built up around the old squire's residential farm and estate, where the Mansion, dating back to 1815, is the central building. The museum's collection consists of boats, individual exhibits, written sources, pictures, other objects of interest and oral traditions recorded from the region's cultural and natural history.

There are a number of historic monuments in the museum grounds from prehistoric times, the Middle Ages and up until the present day. All this goes to show that the Storvågan area played a significant part in North Norwegian coastal culture for a very long time.

From Squire's Mansion to Old People's Home

In 1801, Erik Rønning was given a licence to run Storvågan as a trading post, but it was not until

A quiet Sunday during Storvågan's Golden Age, c. 1890. 2000 fishermen were staying here for the Lofoten Fishery. Here, they are in their Sunday best, and their Lofoten Chests have been placed outside the rorbu cabins. (Photo: Thorstein Brændmo. Narvik Library.)

Caspar Lorch married Rønning's widow in 1811, that the trading post began to flourish. Lorch was a squire who did not much care what methods he had to use to get things done, engaging, amongst other things, in the smuggling of liquor from England. His successor was his son-in-law, Johan Hammond Wolff. Wolff went bankrupt in 1873, but his oldest son took over the business and continued operations at the trading post in Storvågan. There were considerable difficulties in the fishing industry towards the end of the 1800's, and many of the reputable squire dynasties went bankrupt, as did Wolff in Storvågan.

In 1901, the bank, Vaagan Sparebank, took over most of the property and later presented it to the municipality as a gift – whereupon it was almost immediately put to use as an old people's home. By today's standards one might safely say that it was poorly suited to such a role, but it remained as such up until 1975. It was not only the elderly who ended up at the old people's home in Storvågan. Residents also included mentally handicapped people, who were sent there at a relatively tender age, only to spend most of their lives in the old people's home.

The Mansion in Storvågan, then, has borne witness to most aspects of life. Lavish parties were thrown here during the squire's regime, and King Oscar II landed here during his visit to Vågan in 1873. But also many of those who were regarded by society as the lowliest of individuals have also lived their lives here – albeit in anything but luxury.

Wolff's bankruptcy in the late 1800's marked the end of what had been one of our most important fishing stations for 900 years. Archaeological examinations have proven that Storvågan was established on the site of the old North Norwegian mediaeval centre of Vågar, and that there has been a fishing station on the site throughout the entire period, from about the year 1000 AD until the 1900's.

Today, Storvågan is once again of central importance in Lofoten, when it comes to both cultural history and to tourism. The Lofoten Museum sustains the links backwards in time with our own coastal culture, while simultaneously maintaining solid foundations in both Norwegian and European history.

The Vågan Fair

The Vågastemnet, or Vågan Fair, conjures up an atmosphere of history. The name dates back to the Middle Ages, and the fair itself represented a significant economic, political and cultural link

Fine weather was good drying weather for the sails. Here, we see a man and a small boy launching a rowing boat in Rekøykjeila near Kabelvåg.
(Photographer: Thorstein Brændmo. Oslo University Library)

between the north and the south of Norway. The Vågan Fair was held in Vågan (Vågar) every year, starting in the early summer when the fishermen who had taken part in the Lofoten fishery during the winter had returned to take the dried cod down from the fish racks and sell it. All kinds of people assembled here – northerners, southerners and foreigners; the King's men, North Norwegian men of distinction, men of the cloth, and others who wanted to be where it was all happening – not to mention the merchants from Bergen and Trondheim, who came to buy fish and sell wares that were not so easy to get hold of up here in the north. In this way, the Vågan Fair, and thus the borough of Vågan, became the meeting place linking North Norway to the rest of Norway, and to the rest of the world.

Since time immemorial, the Norwegian Arctic cod has made its way down to Lofoten to spawn, and has therefore always been an important resource for the coastal population. What made the Lofoten fishery of such increasing importance was the production of winter-dried cod. The Lofoten fishery takes place at a time of the year when conditions are very favourable for hanging fish out to dry. And there was a need for this dried fish in the Catholic countries of southern Europe during Lent, when eating meat was forbidden and only so-called "white food" was allowed.

This meant that for the Norwegian monarchy, the Lofoten fishery became a very interesting economic proposition, and it therefore developed into a commercial fishery shortly after the year

1000 AD. In this way, the dried cod, or stockfish, became the first Norwegian export commodity of any importance. According to the historians, stockfish from North Norway comprised no less than 80% of total Norwegian exports in the 1300's.

The Vågan Fair was Divided into Three Parts

The mediaeval centre of Vågan developed during the transitional period between the Viking Age and the Middle Ages. In Snorre's "Saga of the Kings", we can read about Asbjørn Selsbane from Trondenes who was killed on his way back from the Vågan Fair in the year 1024 AD. An Icelandic saga, Grette's Saga, tells the story of Grette Åsmundsson who was at the Vågan Fair both in the year 1012 and in 1013.

In the "Saga of Olav Tryggvason", the Viking chieftain Tore Hjort from Vågan is mentioned. According to the saga he was killed at the hands of King Olav Tryggvason himself, in the year 999 AD. Tore Hjort probably lived on the island of Gimsøya, but Gimsøy and Vågan were considered as one during the transitional period from the Viking Age to the Middle Ages. Tore Hjort's death in 999 marked the end of the old chieftain's dynasties in our region. At about the same time, the Lofoten Fishery, or Vågan fishe-

ry as it was then known, began to gain importance as a commercial fishery. The King wanted control over the abundant fisheries in Lofoten and so, in order to distance himself from the reign of the chieftains, he established his centre in Vågan, where the fish were most abundant.

The Vågan Fair was more than just a trade fair. The monarchy, too, wanted to take advantage of the fact that so many people were gathered together in Vågan, and a *Thing*, a legislative and judicial assembly, was established there. The *Thing* was located to Brurberget Rock in the close vicinity of Storvågan. Disagreements were settled at the Thing, and judges passed verdicts on all kinds of crimes. The most famous *Thing* at Brurberget was held in the year 1282 when the so-called "Våga Book" – a special book of law applying to Vågan alone – was repealed. The King's law was to be the one and only law for the entire country. Vågan had its own currency, too, the so-called Vågasilver.

In 1321, archbishop Eiliv visited Vågan and founded an annual North Norwegian clerical assembly. It was here decreed that all churches in North Norway, together with the bishopric of Nidaros, should be represented at the summer fair in Vågan. The idea behind this assembly of the clergy was that all churches in North Norway were to pay 40 fish each to the cathedral in Nidaros, and payment was to be made "at sumarstempno i Vaghom" – during the summertime in Vågan – every year.

Vågan and the Struggle for the Crown

We know that on several occasions Vågan also played an important role in the struggle for royal power. In the Middle Ages it was not always easy to know who had the right to be King. Indeed, at times there were several contenders to the throne, and this could often lead to strife.

In the year 1027, King Olav the Holy ordered mobilisation for war along the entire coast, in order to meet threats from the Danish King, Canute the Mighty. Olav sent Finn Arnesson to North Norway to organise the army there, and Arnesson in turn summoned all the powerful North Norwegians to a meeting in Vågan. Tore Hund from Bjarkøy came too, and a struggle for power developed between Finn Arnesson and Tore Hund.

Tore Hund

Finn Arnesson summoned a "*husting*" – a special court of justice for the warring army. Tore Hund was to answer for the crimes he had commited during his trip to Bjarmeland (northern Russia). Tore had killed the King's envoy,

Karle, and taken a gold necklace from his body. Finn demanded that Tore should return the necklace and pay a fine for killing one of the King's men. Tore paid the fine, but he had managed to conceal most of the valuable load of pelts that he had brought back with him from Bjarmeland, so it turned out to be an inexpensive affair for him. Tore had had a false bottom put in his barrels. He filled the upper part with beer, and when Finn Arnesson took a look in them, he saw only the beer. What he did not see was that most of the barrels were filled with the most precious pelts that Tore was later to take with him to England and sell.

King Øystein in Vågan

There is a statue of King Øystein Magnusson in Kabelvåg. It was erected in 1935 when it was decided to pay tribute to him for founding Vågan. Several different passages from the sagas tell of how Øystein visited Vågan and built a church there, while his brother, Sigurd Jorsalfar was on a pilgrimage in the Holy Land. In one of the passages, it says that Øystein also commanded the building of "rorbu" cabins for the fishermen. However, King Øystein can hardly be attributed with the foundation of Vågan. The reason he came to Vågan was most likely the fact that the place was already of great significance to the monarchy, and he probably came here to strengthen his position in the north.

There was a period of unrest and strife after the death of the Royal brothers Øystein and Sigurd. Norway entered into a state of civil war that lasted for a hundred years. Two of those who were fighting for the kingship, Sigurd Slembe and Magnus the Blind, were staying in the north during the winter of 1138-39. They came to Vågan in the spring of 1139. The only thing that is mentioned of their visit is that they killed Svein the Priest and his two sons.

Towards the end of the civil war, in 1224, Vågan once again played a part in the struggle for royal power. Håkon Håkonsson fought for the kingship against Inge Bårdsson and his half-brother Skule Bårdsson, also known as Skule Jarl. In 1223, Håkon and Skule agreed that North Norway should be under Skule's jurisdiction, and Skule Jarl came to Vågan in 1224 to look after his interests in North Norway. On this occasion, too, one of the King's men was killed in Vågan, and a *Thing* was convened. And once again, many of North Norway's most powerful men assembled at the Vågan Fair.

Documents from the Middle Ages

Official documents are another important written source from the Middle Ages. We call such docu-

ments diplomas. Over half the diplomas written in North Norway before the year 1400, were written in Vågan. All the diplomas from Vågan were written during the winter or summer; that is, during the Vågan Fair. Several of these diplomas tell us that the archbishop of Nidaros himself was present at the Vågan Fair, confirming the important position the Vågan Fair had in the Middle Ages.

One of the diplomas from Vågan provides an account of an extravagant wedding that was held here on the old Norse red letter day of Jakob Våthatt, on July 25, 1335. Ingebjørg Ivarsdotter and Torleif Sigurdsson were married on that day. The diploma describes the dowry that accompanied Ingebjørg into wedlock, and it tells us that the couple were of wealthy stock. No mention is made of the wedding itself, but there is no doubt that it was a major event. No less than four clergymen were present in addition to two of the wealthiest men in North Norway.

Outsiders Arranged the Vågan Fair

It is interesting to note that even though Vågan was the financial, political and religious centre of North Norway, we can find no physical traces of large residences from this period. There is no stone church here like those we

For centuries the warehouse workers balanced stockfish on their barrows at the Bryggen Warehouses in Bergen. (Photo: Wilse, 1907. The Norwegian Folk Museum's photo collection)

find in many other places in the north. Nor is there any evidence to suggest that any significant men of influence have been resident in Vågan, or that the Vicar of Vågan has played any important role during the Vågan Fair. This would seem to imply that outsiders must have organised the Vågan Fair. The archbishop of Nidaros held the Clerical Assembly, the Law Speaker organised the *Thing*, and the merchants of Bergen and Trondheim held a trade fair.

The Vågan of the Middle Ages can therefore hardly be called a township, but it is quite clear that the location was an important centre of trade and had township functions at least during parts of the year.

Age of Decline

Vågan disappears from written sources around the year 1400.

There were probably several reasons for this, of which the most important one was the Black Death – the plague that wrought havoc all over Europe. Trade fairs like the Vågan Fair, where townsmen from Bergen and fishermen from all over Northern Norway all met and mingled, were extremely vulnerable events. The reason why the Vågan Fair became so important was that so many people were congregated in one small area over a short period of time. In the years after 1350, this did not happen any more. The Black Death had hit the North Norwegian production areas, i.e. the fisheries districts; and the townsmen who traded in North Norway, were hit with particular vehemence.

The monarchy, however, tried to keep Vågan on its feet as its North Norwegian centre, for as long as possible. In a decree issued by King Olav Håkonsson in 1384, it says: "We and Our council, bishops, knights and several others are indeed aware that our trading townships of Bergen, Trondheim and Vågan and the other smaller trading posts, are being spoiled and laid waste because seamen are no longer sailing with their wares to the long-established trade fairs ... Firstly, those from Finnmark and Helgeland shall sail to Vågan." Here, then, we have a decree ordering the North Norwegians to trade in Vågan during the summer fair. Further on in the decree it says, "But our townsmen in Bergen shall sail to Vågan, and hold their trade fair there." This supports the theory that the trade fairs were arranged by outsiders.

Such a Royal decree proved futile, however, and the township of Vågan had lost its significance. This is confirmed by reading the "Description of Lofoten and Vesteraalen" written in 1591 by Erik Hansen Schønnebøl who was the bailiff of Lofoten and Vesterålen at that time. He writes that the fishing village of Voge was previously a township but had now become a poor fishing village with "10-12 impoverished beggars."

A Shift in the Centre

After the Black Death, Vågan lost its position as centre of nor-

thern Norway. The settlement itself was still regarded as an important fishing village, and indeed it remained so until towards the end of the 1800's, but apart from this, it was of no greater significance than any other place of a similar nature.

From the mid 1800's, Kabelvåg took over the dominant position that Storvågan had had. This shift in centre from Storvågan to Kabelvåg, one kilometre further to the west, probably took place gradually and over a long period of time. The reasons why Kabelvåg took over the role of centre are still not known in detail. It has been suggested that harbour conditions were better in Kabelvåg than in Storvågan, and that Kabelvåg could therefore accommodate bigger boats, but this is probably not the whole explanation.

On the other hand, when it comes to the subsequent shift in centre from Kabelvåg to Svolvær, around the turn of the century, this can be explained entirely in terms of harbour conditions. The advent of the motor fishing vessel in the coastal fishing fleet led to an increase in the size of boats, and Kabelvåg could not accommodate such vessels. Svolvær, on the other hand, had been endowed with an excellent harbour by the powers that be, and when the Coastal Steamer was established in 1893, Svolvær soon became a port of call.

Gradually, Svolvær developed into a harbour for more or less the entire coastal fleet. This meant that all innovation was located in Svolvær, and Kabelvåg was left to stagnate.

The following passage has been translated from: Elstad, K.: "A Celebrated Wedding in Vågan":

A diploma dating back to 1335 provides us with an account of a momentous wedding that took place in Vågan. The bride was Ingebjørg Ivarsdotter and the bridegroom, Torleiv Sigurdsson. No less than four clergymen from Trondenes, Steigen, Borge and Vågan made sure that the couple were properly married. We can see from the dowry that accompanied Ingebjørg into wedlock, that the couple were of wealthy origins. At that time, and for a long time afterwards, material value was assessed in "cow-values", and a cow was worth a great deal indeed.

Torleiv had chosen well. Ingebjørg's dowry included extensive landed properties, a large consignment of stockfish and 10 cows. In addition to this, the bride owned many beautiful things: patterned, woven tablecloths and rugs, embroidered pillows and silk pillows, quilts with, amongst other things, silver and gold embroidery, bedclothes, clothing and ornaments. The estimated total value of these things amounted to 80 cow-values! Ingebjørg was most certainly accustomed to grand ways and a life of luxury. Amongst other things, she had a shawl and a fur hat that were each worth one cow-value! She also had a piece of gold-plated silver jewellery worth 4 cow values. Her fur capes were valued at 5 and 6 cow-values, one of them was of grey leather, and another was made from squirrel furs and sable.

Their contact with European countries is demonstrated by the textiles of foreign origin that are listed in the dowry. The list includes German mattress covers, an English woollen blanket, German tablecloths and towels and a chest with iron ornamentation from Germany. Several exclusive textiles have French names, including a Salun (Chalons) rug, a Kaprun (chaperon) cape and a Syrkot (surcote) coat. Only the rich had clothes in vivid colours. The diploma tells us that Ingebjørg had several tunics and gowns in red, blue and spotted colours. On the dowry list we can also find several fur hats, a silk hood and a violet hood with white ermine fur. Ingebjørg must have been quite a sight indeed, strutting around old Vågar in her finery.

Ingebjørg's Dowry

The History of Art in Lofoten

Gunnar Berg – Lofoten Lad and Painter

It was Gunnar Berg who once and for all put Lofoten on the agenda of Norwegian pictorial art. He was born in Svolvær in 1863. His father, squire and mer-chant Berg, was a wise man. He had probably wanted his oldest son to take over the business, but let him instead cultivate his art-istic talents. At the age of 12, Gunnar Berg left for Bergen and the Cathedral School there, but it was his private drawing and paint-

"Svolvær harbour" – painting by Gunnar Berg. In an obituary, the author Bernt Lie said: "It is no exaggeration when I say that Gunnar Berg loved the Nordland-type boats." Gunnar Berg's portrayals of the environment are full of detail and provide valuable documentation of contemporary life in the harbour. The painting is now on display at Lofoten House, Henningsvær.

ing classes that he lived for. He was determined to become an artist. At the age of twenty he went to Germany to study for two years at the Dusseldorf Academy of Art. In 1886, he moved to Berlin and took part in several field trips to Paris. Gunnar Berg painted motifs from Lofoten, and in particular, his beloved Svolvær during the winter. He took part in a number of exhibitions both in Norway and abroad – and was well received by critics. In 1889 he had his first separate exhibition where he presented no less than 146 paintings.

"Sorely Missed"

Even as a boy, Gunnar Berg had been troubled by pain in his right foot, and in 1887 he underwent an operation. Further operations followed before the doctors finally diagnosed cancer. In the autumn of 1893 his leg had to be amputated. During the winter of that same year, in Berlin, he became very ill, at first with influenza and then with pneumonia. In a final letter to his brother John, he writes, " ... I think my suffering is more than my body can take, or else the whole thing is just a bad dream." His illness grew worse, and father and brother left for Berlin. They arrived on the night before Christmas Eve, but on that very same morning, Gunnar Berg had passed away.

He was buried on the islet of Gunnar-holmen, close by the island of Svinøya in Svolvær.

His brush was active for just ten years, but when he died, he left an enormous number of works behind him. In his studio in Svolvær, there were about 600 paintings, sketches and studies. One of his major works, "The Battle of Trollfjord" can be seen today in the Town Hall in Svolvær. Gunnar Berg leads the field of North Norwegian painters. Today, he is referred to as a "richly gifted" painter who could have reached "the zenith of art, had his sands of time not run out so swiftly ..."

"Difficult – difficult to paint this!"

It is the light, the colours and the scenery that attract the artists. But Lofoten has not always been described as beautiful and picturesque. In 1827, district governor G. Blom wrote:

"Lofoten is so devoid of natural beauty as is at all possible. There can be no question as to which of these places is the most beautiful, but the ugliest is without doubt Sund in Flakstad."

Times change. Towards the end of the 1800's, artists began to discover the Northlands – and Lofoten. The famous Norwegian painter, Christian Krohg, came to Lofoten and Svolvær in about 1896. He wanted to visit the place where "Gunnar Berg was born, lived and is sorely missed." During his winter visit, he wrote: "Difficult – difficult to paint this! To portray the height, the grandeur, and Nature's inexorable, merciless tranquillity and indifference. But it is possible, and the task is a great one."

Lofoten – A Magnet

The scope of art and artists is vast. All art forms are represented here, but painters have always been the dominant group. Many artists come to the islands on short stays, but a large group of artists also belong to Lofoten's permanent population. Every island has its artists, some are famous and well-established, with their own galleries and sales premises, others can be found in the attic and down in the cellar, or in a rented "rorbu" cabin. Some advertise, some have signposts by the roadside - and others you only "hear about" from friends – someone who went there last year ...

"Klippenborg" in Svolvær

The history of art in Lofoten has its nucleus in Svolvær and Vågan. The Artist's House in Svolvær – on the island of Svinøya – is one of the oldest art institutions in the county of Nordland. Its roots go back to the 1920's and 30's. At that time, the merchant's daughter, Alfhild Størmer Olsen was a central figure in the artistic community in Svolvær. She was unmarried, had travelled a great deal, and often had guests at her house, "Klippenborg". She let artists stay there for a small fee – and they came, and they worked. Many Swedish artists in particular, like Hans Albin Amelin and Sven Erixson, found their way to Miss Størmer Olsen's "artist's house". Significant Norwegian artists there included Axel Revold and Harald Dal.

A Studio with Room for Two

In 1910, the Swedish painter Anna Boberg built a tiny studio on Kjeøya on the approach to Svolvær harbour. There was hardly room enough for two painters at a time there, but there was great joy when, in the early thirties, it was donated to Swedish and Norwegian painters. It was demolished by the Germans during the war, however, to make room for a gun emplacement. Electric power station manager, Kjeld Langfeldt of Svolvær, was an eager amateur painter and had good contact with the artists. He recognised the need for an Artist's House. Boberg's studio was gone, and Miss Størmer

Kaare Espolin Johnson: "Røstbåter"
– Boats from Røst.

Olsen's activities were frequently visited.

Langfeldt had the idea of an Artist's House on the island of Svinøya. By 1953 the house had been built with the help of private capital and Swedish and Norwegian state funding. The House is complete with bedsits and studios for Swedish and Norwegian artists.

Art Centre and Young Artists

The North Norwegian Artist's Centre, which was established in 1979, can also be found in Svinøya. In 1985, the Centre's premises were finally complete and ready for use, and the institution was named the Vågan Centre of Art. A wide range of exciting exhibitions is arranged here.

The Kabelvåg School of Art was opened in 1983, providing a basic curriculum for pictorial artists and craftsmen. The school is of

The Espolin Gallery

Innumerable Lofoten artists might be named in such a context as this. Yet, this time, suffice to mention a North Norwegian artist who exercised his great talents throughout the course of his long life, and who lived to experience the opening of his own gallery, the Espolin Gallery in Storvågan, Kabelvåg. Kaare Espolin Johnson (1907-1994) was a pictorial artist who visited Lofoten many times. His works unite North Norwegian reality with superstition, the fabulous with the mystical. The Espolin Gallery exhibits about 100 of his works.

Stamsund – Children's Art and Puppets

The foundations of our personalities are laid in childhood. A journey to Stamsund on the island of Vestvågøy will lead you to Vestvågøy Children's Art School. Children's art is taken seriously here, with tuition and exhibitions.

The Children's Art School also takes play seriously. So too, does Nordland Puppet Workshop, also in Stamsund. The most incredible puppets see the light of day in the workshop – and strange, exciting and exotic plays are frequently performed.

great significance to the recruitment of new artists and is a springboard to the academies of art.

Vestvågøy

– A Miniature Continent

Vestvågøy is the maiden of Lofoten: wild and wonderful, fertile and versatile. You will find it all here – geographical diversity including everything from beaches and plains to marshes and stark mountain peaks. There are sheer mountains on all sides, with the tallest ones to the south and west. And between the mountains, across the middle of the island, there are fertile valleys that provide Lofoten with its most important agricultural areas.

The Sea and the Land

Many people live in built up areas on the island of Vestvågøy. The municipal centre, Leknes, is undergoing constant development, yet even so, there are still viable rural areas where people live in tiny hamlets, fishing villages and other more rustic communities like those of Eggum and Unstad.

Fishing and farming are the most important trades in the borough. There are a number of active, traditional fishing villages in Vestvågøy, like Ballstad, Tangstad, Mortsund and Steine, and furthermore, the headquarters of the Lofoten Trawler Co. can be found in the fishing village of Stamsund. Fish farming is a trade undergoing considerable development, both when it comes to production and to research. On land, a considerable number of people are employed in the agricultural sector. The Vestvågøy Dairy has many local suppliers, and the Lofoten Hospital is another major provider of jobs. Other trades include retailing, service industries and the engineering industry. The island of Vestvågøy is also the centre of education in western Lofoten.

New Borough on Historic Ground

Up until 1963, the island consisted of four municipalities called Borge, Buksnes, Hol and Valberg. Consequently, the borough of Vestvågøy is a relatively new municipality, but nonetheless one with long-standing traditions.

Historic monuments are numerous and readily available, ranging from the colossal Chieftain's Homestead in Borg, to the grave of the woman, "Gyda" in Sund.

Borg on the Island of Vestvågøy

Have you ever wished you had a time machine? One like you have seen in Donald Duck comics, that takes Donald and the boys on the most incredible adventures in both the past and the future? At the Viking Museum of Borg in Vestvågøy, the archaeologists have actually managed to construct a time machine, although not like the one in Donald Duck. In this time machine, your own imagination is the engine, but the Viking Museum does supply some powerful fuel.

The Find

It all began one summer's day in 1981 when a farmer from Borg, Frik Harald Bjerkli, was ploughing on the top of the Borg plateau. The plough churned forth rich, dark soil and Frik realised he had discovered something special. People who could recall how things had been way back in time, before they began to plough on Borg hill, remembered that they had seen strange embankments up there, but no-one had thought any more of it. An archaeologist who visited the site in 1890 had also noticed these em-

bankments, but had been more interested in the magnificent burial mounds on the neighbouring hillside. Consequently, the embankments remained untouched.

I imagine you are now wondering what these embankments might have been. The same interest was shared by the first archaeologists that arrived on the scene, after Frik had ploughed the field. The skilful amateur archaeologist, Kåre Ringstad from Vestvågøy, realised straight away that this dark soil concealed the remnants of a prehistoric settlement, and he therefore contacted the archaeologists in Tromsø. It was they who, shortly afterwards, could be seen making their way across the fields, backs bent in search of finds. Suddenly, pieces of broken glass appeared, and the archaeologists could not believe their eyes when they saw that the shards were decorated with pure gold foil. Such finds were previously unknown in Norway, and to find a similar occurrence, one had to go all the way to Central Europe. They realised that the old embankments, which after years of ploughing were now only barely visible in the field, had to have been the turf walls of a prehistoric building.

The Excavations

This was the start of excavations that lasted all the way up until 1989. In the course of these 7 years, archaeologists from all over Scandinavia uncovered

The Homestead as we believe it may have looked. (Photo: Vebjørn Storeide)

the largest Viking Age building ever found in Scandinavia. And this, Scandinavia's largest Viking Age building, was of quite some size indeed, measuring approximately 83 metres in length and about 9 metres across.

The Chieftain's House

Not only was it a large building, it had also been lived in for a very long time. Today, we think that 80 year old houses are ancient and out of date. Many of us would prefer to demolish them and build new ones. The building at Borg was in use for nearly 500 years! During this period of time it was altered and extended several times. The oldest stage dates back to the period we call the Age of Migration (400-500 AD), at the time when the Roman Cæsars ruled southern Europe. The main stage of the building dates back to Merovingian times (c. 570 – 800 AD) and the early Viking Age (800-900 AD). By that time

the Roman Empire had long since waned, and the Germanic tribe known as the Franks dominated European politics.

The Chieftain's Homestead

During these 500 years, the people of Borg continued to settle and build their houses – while elsewhere, empires rose and fell. Perhaps you are thinking that Borg and the rest of Lofoten were real out-of-the-way places that were never affected by such major upheaval. This is, however, not the case at all! It is not without reason that the residence in Borg is hitherto the biggest building of its kind to be found in Scandinavia. A chieftain or prince lived here with his wife, children, servants, slaves and perhaps some of his men. The chieftain's men were free men who swore allegiance to him. This chieftain had contacts with princes and rich people all over Europe. Everything from international politics to the prevailing fashions of the time was followed with vigilant eyes.

How do we know this, you might ask. The building found by the archaeologists was divided into several rooms. In the middle of the house we find the hall, which was the parlour, banqueting hall and chapel of the time. In the north-eastern corner of the hall, the archaeologists found pieces of glass and ceramics from France and England. In the ceramic jug, the chieftain has most probably had the finest of wines, and perchance they celebrated the main festivities or other major events by drinking mead and ale from Frankish glasses.

2 cm

The top of a gold pointer. (Photo: Olga Kvalheim. Tromsø Museum)

They also brought back jewellery from England, and a tiny golden pointer might well have served as a souvenir from a successful campaign.

"Icons" in Gold Leaf

In the same corner in which the glasses were found, the archaeologists dug out small pictures in gold leaf. These golden charms show a couple embracing each other. Such figures had previously only been found on large landed estates where chieftains or men of distinction lived. Furthermore, they are found almost exclusively in the hall.

Archaeological finds and written sources both indicate that such golden charms were normally laid in the soil near the prince's high seat, or throne. This high seat was a large bench or chair that was raised above the other benches. Here, the chieftain and his wife would sit. Perhaps the gold leaf icons were laid down in the house as a kind of symbolic foundation stone. The embracing couple may represent the mythical, primordial couple that were the origin of the chieftain's lineage. Several well known skaldic lays from the Viking Age, like *Ynglingatal* and *Hålogtal*, tell of such a mythical wedding between a god and a "*Jotunkvinne*", or female giant, that was to be the origin of the chieftain's ancestry.

Borg – A Regional Centre

For a long time, archaeologists had suspected that there might be a chieftain's homestead in Borg. They knew that the site of some very large boathouses was to be found close by. These boathouses had probably housed swift and beautiful ships of the same type as the Gokstad ship from the county of Vestfold. Ships like these were the vessels of prominent people. The remains of a site where the buildings had been laid out in a circle, or perhaps a horseshoe formation, had also been found. Such buildings were probably not ordinary houses or farms. Archaeologists believe that they were more likely to have been the site of a local parliament or *Thing*, military barracks for the chieftain's men, or a meeting place for visiting noblemen. Many large burial mounds have also been found in the vicinity of Borg. At Eltoft, a few kilometres away, a grave was found containing one of the most magnificent swords ever found in North Norway. All this would seem to indicate that Borg was a regional centre.

The Eltoft sword, one of the finest sword finds from North Norway. (Photo: Risë Taylor. Tromsø Museum)

logical finds show that the Sami, or Lapps, also played an important role in such operations. It was largely they who caught the fur-bearing animals and reindeer that were of such importance to the chieftains as barter. Some believe that the chieftains offered the Sami protection, and that they therefore had to reciprocate by presenting the chieftains with precious gifts. Others, however, believe that the chieftain and his men had to travel to the mainland and barter with the Sami at annual meetings. Whatever the case, this just goes to show how important the Sami way of life and their products were, in helping the chieftain obtain his much coveted commodities.

The Prosperity of the Chieftain

So how could a chieftain and his kin from Lofoten be so wealthy and powerful that they could acquire precious objects from near and afar? North Norway had riches that the princes of Europe were more than interested in obtaining. The chieftain or his men got hold of walrus tusks (ivory), walrus-skin ropes, eider down, and all kinds of precious pelts and skins. Many of these wares they fetched from the wilderness themselves, but some written sources and a number of archaeo-

The chieftain himself, or some of his closest men, may have travelled to southern Scandinavia as often as once a year to barter goods. He spent a lot of time and many gifts maintaining his friendship with the other chieftains. Time was also spent catching fish, seals, whales and game with which to feed his men and his household.

The Lady of the House

Because of her husband's travels, the lady of the homestead was a very important person on the farm. She was responsible for operations there, and for house-keeping and cooking, all of which were very important tasks. Hence the lady of the house acquired considerable power and esteem. In the Viking Age, the power of the chieftain was not absolute. He and his wife supplemented each other, and were equals. This can also be seen on the tiny golden foil motifs. These pictures, that probably illustrate the origins of the chieftain's lineage, show both a man and a woman. It is therefore apparent that both the man and the woman were important in ensuring that the prince's lineage should evolve and become the strongest. With the advent of Christianity towards the end of the Viking Age, everything became focused on the man.

Inside the main hall, just next to the high seat, the archaeologists found spinning wheels, loom bobs, and bits of soapstone pots. The spinning wheels and loom bobs were used to make textiles. All these things belong in the category of Viking Age women's work. The fact that they were found near the throne might imply that women's work was greatly appreciated. The throne was indeed the most important place in the entire house. Guests who were received by the lady of the house and the chieftain on their throne were therefore also able to witness the pride of the farm: the magnificent textiles that had been woven by the lady of the house.

The End of an Era

By about the year 900, the chieftain's residence had been abandoned. This was round about the time of the great migration from Norway to Iceland. Perhaps the Chieftain of Borg had fallen out with one of the mighty kings in the south, so that his entire family had been forced to flee the country? To be sure, it was at about this time that the first kings of Norway began their attempts to break the power of the old chieftains of Hålogaland. It was not only the princes of central Europe that were interested in the riches of the Chieftain of Borg.

The fall of Borg marks the end of the age of the chieftains in Norway.

Borg is Both Ordinary and Unique

The Chieftain's Homestead in Borg was both quite unique and quite ordinary. It was unique because it was only chieftains that could pursue such a lifestyle. The fine arts were cultivated here, and there was often good food on the table. The chieftain was inundated with news and precious objects from far and wide, and had friends and contacts all over northern Europe.

For most people, however, life was quite different. They struggled and toiled to make ends meet. Just as they were up until modern times, most of the inhabitants were fishermen-farmers, the men fishing and hunting seals and birds when they were not working on the farm. The women took care of the housekeeping and the everyday chores on the farm. However, life had its moments for them, too: like when a child was born, when the catch was good, and when the cows yielded an abundance of milk. And maybe the farmer had joined the chieftain on a raid along foreign coasts, too, and been given a ring of silver in reward. This would follow him to his grave, along with his axe and spear, when the time came. His wife would spend her vacant moments planning their daughter's wedding. The silver ring should be part of the dowry, she thought. It was only fitting for her daughter. In the area surrounding Borg, we find a number of ruins of the farms of such people, showing the great contrast between their lives and that of the chieftain.

The Chieftain's homestead was also quite ordinary. There were similar chieftains with their princely kindred, all along the Norwegian coast. There were similar principalities in both Buksnesfjord on the other side of Vestvågøya, in Steigen on the mainland, near Stokmarknes in Hadsel, and on the island of Andøya. Nor was Borg necessarily among the biggest and most powerful of these. Near Buksnesfjord you will find the same type of courtyard in the form of a circle or horseshoe, one of the biggest burial grounds in North Norway, and the biggest boathouse site we know of in this country. Written sources describing the later part of the Viking Age, report that in times of war, the people of the area around the Vestfjord had to provide the biggest boat in the whole of Norway. And of those we know of, only this boathouse site is big enough to have housed such a boat. The fact that boats of this size were moored near the Buksnesfjord, serves to show how important a place it was.

The Viking Museum

Has your time machine begun to work, but you have not quite taken off yet? Then you should pay a visit to the Viking Museum in Borg. The entire chieftain's residence we have discussed here has been reconstructed in a full-scale replica. You can enter the residential part and see how the archaeologists imagine daily life was lived on the chieftain's farm. Tall columns support the roof, the great fireplace in the middle of the floor provides heat and light. Along the walls you can catch a glimpse of chests and tables that have been put to one side. If you are lucky, you may meet a couple of the women of the farm, weaving a new dress for the lady of the house. Or perhaps you will get to taste a piece of the bread they are baking. Go into the banqueting hall and admire the high seat. It is richly adorned with engraved heads and is raised well above the other benches. Perhaps your inner eye will catch a glimpse of the chieftain and his wife as they receive a well-to-do farmer from Buksnes?

In the part of the main building that was used as a barn, a major exhibition has been built up, where finds from Borg are on display. You can see those strange gold leaf pictures, as small as fingernails and as thin as paper, yet even so, powerful symbols of their time. You can see the rest of the riches that the Vikings brought back with them from far off countries. Splendid burial finds from Vestvågøy show how the rich lived and dressed. And at the far end of the exhibition, you can see how the barn itself may originally have looked.

Perhaps the boathouse in the Buksnesfjord looked like this one, too. On the adjacent waters, a replica of the Gokstad ship is moored. The Chieftain of Borg will also have had such a ship. On the way down to the boat, if your eyesight serves you well, you will be able to see the old fields where the Vikings grew their corn. Domestic animals of the same kinds kept by the Vikings are at pasture out in the fields.

You are a Time Machine

Do you feel that your time machine has brought you back to the Viking Age? Or are there too many tourists there wearing trainers and a walkman, and ruining your enjoyment of it? You must remember that the Viking Museum only provides the fuel for your time machine. Only your own imagination can take you back to the past. Sit down in a quiet place and close your eyes. Imagine that beneath your feet, lie the remnants of thousands of years of endless history. History that is waiting for you to discover it, and to pass it on.

Take the time to stroll down to the Borgpollen fjord, where a Viking Age boathouse has been reconstructed.

The remains of the Homestead in Borg.
(Sketch, Borg: Basic plan of chieftain's homestead showing division of rooms. By D. Kaldal Mikkelsen.)

Full speed ahead. The Viking Ship Lofotr *is a replica of the Gokstad ship. The chieftain of Borg would probably have had such a magnificent vessel. Perhaps there were even bigger and finer ships at Holnesset in the Buksnesfjorden? (Photo: Vebjørn Storeide.)*

Perhaps you will hear the joyful shouts of the men returning from the hunt, or the laughter of the chieftain's daughter at a hopeless suitor. It's all up to you. You have a full tank, turn on the ignition of your time machine – and take off!

The Viking Museum of Borg is the Borough of Vestvågøy's contribution to the project "Footprints in the North – A Guide to a Thousand Years of Cultural Monuments in North Norway and Namdalen."

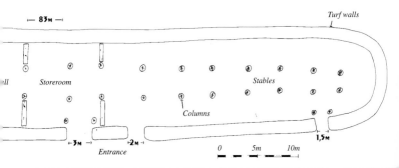

Women's Lives and Women's Graves Along the Coast During the Iron Age

Burial finds constitute one of the most important sources of our knowledge of the past. Large numbers of Iron Age finds have been made, providing us with important information about society at that time. Most early Iron Age burial finds date back to Roman times and the Age of Migration (200 – 500 AD). Most of our burial finds from the late Iron Age, are of Viking Age origin (800-1050 AD). From the number of graves that have been found, it is clear that not everybody was honoured with a burial mound. It was probably only important members of the clan or of society that were buried in such a way. Normally, we imagine that it was the men who held the most important positions in society, like chieftain and leader. Judging from burial finds, however, this is a notion that may well be debated.

Iron Age graves show that also a great number of women were given such honourable burials. There is even evidence to suggest that during the early Iron Age, the majority of those buried in burial mounds were, in fact, women. This number decreases towards the Viking Age, however, but even so, there were still a large number of women who were laid to rest in burial mounds.

Objects Found in Women's Graves

Women were often buried together with a large number of artefacts and personal effects. Such things can tell us something of people's conception of death. They might also tell us something of the position the deceased had in society. One thing is for sure, the objects found in graves of this kind were often rare, precious and beautiful things, things that we assume with a reasonable degree of certainty were not readily available to everyone. Women's graves from the Iron Age sometimes contained such beautiful and precious objects, and this contributes to our belief that the persons buried there had held important positions in society and in the clan.

One such wealthy woman's grave from the late Iron Age was found at Sund on the island of Vestvågøy in the Lofoten Islands. The woman had been buried with two bronze, oval-shaped brooches designed to hold her costume up. Between them, a string of pearls had been hung and 9 of the pearls were found in the grave. In addition to this, she had been equipped with a bronze ring-brooch and a silver ring. The remains of a ring of jet were also found (made from jet quarried in England), possibly belonging to an arm ring. The woman also had several everyday artefacts with her in the grave. She was buried together with a pair of iron scissors, a weaving batten of whalebone, and a bone knife which was probably used to work skins. There were also the remains of what might have been a knife.

Woman's Role in the Iron Age

What role did these coastal women play during the Iron Age? A lot of evidence indicates that they played a major role in family life and on the farm. Perhaps it had been their responsibility to look after the family and the farm, while the men were to a greater extent involved in operations at sea, or in fishing. The remains of boathouses dating back throughout the entire Iron Age, suggest that the sea was an important resource.

Such a division of labour between man and woman was the tradition on the farms along the coast of Northern Norway for a long time. It is very likely that this pattern had already been established during the Iron Age. Such a division of responsibilities will have made women respectable and dominant figures in social life, particularly in a society that was to such a large extent based around the farm.

Burial finds from the Viking Age indicate that more emphasis had now been placed on the man's role than had been the case during the early Iron Age, but that women still played an important role in society. We know, from amongst other things, the Sagas, that there were female religious leaders during the Viking Age, the so-called "volver", or sibyls. These were prophetesses who could see into the future, and they were highly esteemed. Such women may well have had great political powers by way of their religious position.

Women were often buried together with their jewellery. The ceramic beads and the bone comb pictured abovewere found in a grave in Unstad on the island of Vestvågøy.
(Photo and source: Borge og Valberg Bygdebok, Vol. I, Bodø 1982)

VESTVÅGØY MUSEUM

THE OLD SCHOOL

The old school in Fygle houses the Vestvågøy Museum, and there is still a lot for us to learn in this tall, yellow building that dates back to 1898, and served as a schoolhouse for sixty years.

After climbing the steps and entering the classroom on the left, we encounter a school room in which parents, grandparents and great grandparents will find many familiar things.

To be sure, we can even find the long table from the time when the school service was mobile, moving around from home to home. And we can literally follow school history along the rows of desks up to the most recent Formica ones from our own times. Many visitors will recognise their old "ABC" or their reading and arithmetic books, whereas fewer will remember the old stone slabs for which you needed a slate pen to write on. During the first few decades, the children had to buy their own slate pens and books themselves. They were sold here in the classroom – to those who could afford them.

Pupils, teachers and janitor. (c. 1912) The boys are wearing knickerbockers and the girls are wearing pinafore dresses. (Vestvågøy museum.)

On the wall there are two maps that were important to the world of the old school: the ancient map of Palestine, which had to be learned by heart, and the more recent local history map of Vestvågøy, where a drawing of the Coastal Steamer represents the way out into the world at large. One can also go on imaginary travels with the help of the globe on the teacher's desk, a globe that shows the names of countries and borders that many will long since

have forgotten. The various types of apparatus and old wall charts on show were also helpful aids in the spreading of knowledge.

Reading Aloud, and the Smell of Wet Wool

Here in the classroom, it's as though you can almost hear the uniform drone of reading aloud and the recitation of verses from the psalms. When the psalms were sung, the teacher would accompany the children on the monochord, a simple one-stringed musical instrument. Lars Olsen Eidhammer, who was teacher here during the first 30 years of the school's history, had passed his exams in "Musical Theory and Playing the Monochord" at the teacher training college. Later, the singing of hymns was accompanied by the harmonium.

The old petroleum lamp that once sizzled out white light across the classroom, accompanied by the roar of the stove, is still hanging from the ceiling. It must have been a pleasant room to come to on dark, cold mornings, after a long walk to school. On entering the classroom, one might take a swig of water from the ladle that was shared by everyone, and soon the air would be full of the smell of wet wool from the children's woolly socks and overcoats. There were many children in each class. In the year 1900, there were no less than 36 pupils in the first form at Fygle School.

"Fighting for their Lives"

Here, as elsewhere out in the country, combined classes, consisting of several age groups together, were a common phenomenon. During this century's first couple of decades, the children attended "rotation" school. Each rotation period lasted for two to three weeks, after which the children had two or three weeks off, while other children used the desks. During the winter fishing season, however, all the older boys, between the ages of 11 and 15, were allowed time off school so that they could work as *cooking lads* in the fishermen's cabins. They had to catch up on their school work later. Similar arrangements were made for the girls towards the end of spring, in order that they might earn money towards confirmation clothes for themselves or their sisters.

Altogether, the school year lasted 12-14 weeks.

The school, then, had to adapt to a certain extent, to the fisherman-farmers' struggle to make a living. And sometimes, the children simply had to stay at home and work.

In the "Report on Buksnes School 1896–1900," it says:

"A considerable portion of the population are fighting for their lives and have thus been forced to put their children to work at home in a number of ways.
However, it would seem that more and more people are realising that school is a blessing, since more and more children have obtained their own reading and learning books."

However, not all parents saw the point of sending their children to school.

From 1997, the other classroom on the ground floor will house theme exhibitions based on the history of education. In the meantime, the museum will present the subject of "self-sufficiency" here, displaying important aspects of the pupils' everyday life at home. The knowledge and skills they learned here were by no means inferior to those learnt at school.

The Teacher's Residence

While the building was serving as a schoolhouse, part of the first floor was used for lessons in woodwork and handiwork, and part as the teacher's residence.

The furnishings in the teacher's residence are probably rather more expensive than one would imagine Mr. Eidhammer, who taught here until 1923, would have been able to afford. In 1900, he had an annual salary of 902 kroner. Compared to the price of flour, that would give him the equivalent of an annual salary of 23,000 kroner in 1995 (approx. 12% of an average teacher's salary today). However, in conjunction with the school, there were farm lands that were tended by the teacher, and he also worked as municipal accountant. The room has been maintained in middle-class style with neo-rococo furniture from the 1800's, a pipe holder, a mirror with a shelf beneath it, a moonshine lamp and a bookcase. The plaque with the inscription "Lift in unison and succeed in carrying, the people forth to future glory" seems suitable in a teacher's home, as does the framed photograph of the members of the 1905 cabinet, together with the wall embroidery of the flag and the Norwegian lion.

The Woodwork, Handwork and Meeting Room

The schoolhouse was not only a place of learning, it was also a meeting place for national day celebrations and Christmas parties, and for many years it was also the meeting place of the municipal council. When there was no hammering or sewing going on there, the big room on the first floor was used for sober meetings of the Council and the mediation board. Between 1919 and 1963, the elected members of the Hol Municipal Council voted on all kinds of issues here. One day the salary of the manager of the poor house might have been brought up for discussion, next time it might have been the handing out of cheap flour to the poor, the port of call for the coastal steamer, the appointment of a tuberculosis committee, the building of a church, the licensing of premises, the employment of a doctor and nurse, the water supply, or any number of other topics. We might mention that automobiles were considered such a major traffic problem in 1920, that for a time a ban was imposed on motoring from 8.30 until 11.30 every morning.

Until the museum has completed its exhibition on the history of the municipal administration, the "council chambers" will display, amongst other things, the kitchen work, textile work, shoe-making, and cooper's work of the past.

The Shed and the "Rorbu" Cabin in the School Yard

In the school yard, there was a shed with an outside toilet, a stove for warming the water to wash the floors, and storage space for the peat and other heating fuel that was carried in by horses through the wide, gaping doors.

Today, the old "rorbu" cabin out in the yard is far away from its original location in the harbour of the fishing village of Ure. But by having a look inside, school children and other visitors to the museum can catch a glimpse of the every day conditions experienced by, amongst others, the cooking lads during those winter months when they were absent from school.

This is a double "rorbu" cabin, built in 1834 to accommodate the crew of 4 boats. The rooms were not only for resting in, but were also for working in, and in each cabin, 8-10 men lived and worked together side by side for 2–3 months. When you go in, you enter the "cabin door", a kind of entrance hall where the fishermen kept the tackle they needed. Here, you will find nets and longline tubs, the tools they used for

This net float from Vestvågøy Museum is quite a little sculpture. Man and wife fishing together. The floats were used to show the location of nets and to keep them afloat. (Photo: L.Selnes)

gathering shells for bait, the cod liver oil pan they boiled the fish liver in, and lots more . In the actual "rorbu" room itself, the fishermen slept and ate. Here, too, food was cooked, nets were mended, and wet clothes were hung up to dry. In the broad bunk beds hanging just below the ceiling, two men slept in one bunk, lying close together beneath the boat rugs that their wives or mothers had spent hours weaving.

If you study the fishing tackle closely, you will see that the fishermen were also skilful craftsmen, and many clearly had artistic abilities – and the energy to put them to use, too. Hearts and patterns have been carved into simple everyday pieces of tackle, and one of the net floats is a veritable sculpture. During the summer season, you can see demonstrations of how they made nets, snell for their longlines, and string covers for their glass floats.

THE FISHERMAN'S FARM IN SKAFTNES

Vestvågøy Museum's second department is situated in beautiful surroundings in a tiny bay amid fjord and mountains at Skaftnes between the villages of Sennesvik and Ure. The Museum has taken over the farm with all its inventory and is therefore able to provide us with an insight into life here since the 1860's, when the farmhouse was built, and up to the present day.

As you stand on the beach on a clear summer's day overlooking the white, low-lying Nordland-type house with the sun twinkling in the tiny windowpanes in front of linen curtains, the setting is simply idyllic. The house seems small in comparison to the red-painted warehouse and the large boathouse. Behind the boathouse you will find the smithy; a barn built in 1939 was also a part of the farm.

A man called Nils Nilsen built the house and in 1870 he sold it to Hans Pedersen and Maren Lorentsdatter. Hans was a fisherman and the captain of a boat. Their oldest son, Lorentz, took over the farm from his parents. His wife, Kristine Samsonsdotter, died only 34 years old, and Lorentz remarried, this time to Hansine Kristiansen. It is said of Hansine that she always let travellers stay on the farm and

The fisherman's farm of Skaftnes in Sennesvik. Those living here were probably better off than most. They made a living from fishing and farming, and in the warehouse they bought fish and ran a little shop. (Photo: Runar Klæboe Eidissen.)

would not let them leave until they had eaten, or been given something to take with them. The children who came to Skaftnes to buy milk were always fed.

Lorentz had eleven children altogether, of whom the three oldest emigrated to America. His son Magnus, from the first marriage, took over the farm and lived there together with his half brother, Karl.

Fishing and Hunting

Those who lived here were probably considerably better off than most people, but even so, the house and its contents provide us with a good impression of life and livelihood on the average fisherman's farm. The owners here concentrated mainly on fishing. They fished from their own boats, were also fish buyers and had their own fish racks. Lorentz started a small shop in his ware-

house, too, where the fishermen could buy the basic necessities for fishing. Some fishermen also had lodgings in the attic of the farmhouse – perhaps they worked on Lorentz's fishing boat as hired hands.

The great, stone-walled boathouse alone gives us some indication of the importance of fishing for the economy here on the farm. Today, if you go in, amid the smell of salt and tar, you will find about 15 small boats in this spacious room, but in the 1850's it was built to house the biggest of the Nordland-type boats, the *fembøringen*, which was 12-13 metres long. Today, there is only one other boathouse of this kind left on the island, in Eggum. Various types of fishing tackle also tell their own story.

Along the shore, you can see the remains of rectangular stone formations where the fish were collected when the boats came to land, and in the warehouse you will find many exciting articles reflecting the variety of activities and the utilisation of resources on the farm. In addition to the small general store, there is a tiny, but complete carpenter's workshop. In the attic, where the great winch hauled up fish and salt in bygone times, we find barrel hoops, cod nets, timber logs, seal skins, dog skins, oil skins and fox traps. An enormous baking trough bears witness to the fact that many mouths were fed on the farm.

It would seem that the M/V "Bogtind", a 42 foot fishing boat from 1917, will also become part of the environment in Skaftnes. It is owned by the Museum and the local Coast Association, who also hold their meetings in the warehouse.

The Home

On the way up to the farmhouse, we pass the garden with its perennials dating back to the days of great grandmother. The Gardening Association has been helpful in recreating the scene.

Entering the house is like dropping in on the past. This is a home where commodities were not just used up and thrown away, but where everything was taken care of. On the ground floor we pass through the entrance hall and into the kitchen. The open hearth, with a chimney hook to hang the cauldron on, leads the imagination way back in time, while the radio on the shelf above the kitchen counter returns us to our own time.

Beyond the kitchen we find the chamber, or bedroom, where a modern toilet and shower have been installed.

The brothers Karl and Magnus, who were both unmarried, were the last to live here on a permanent basis, and both of them have had rooms named after them. The entire "Karlsstua" room – and not just the doors as was the norm – has been painted using a special technique to make the surfaces resemble more "nobler" types of wood, in this case oak. In the corner, we find a *Pomor* cabinet – a memento from the days of bartering with Russian fishermen. On the other side of the room, the stove from Wingaard's iron foundry towers up, decorated with frills of wrought iron. Contact with the world at large was as might be expected, but "Home, Sweet Home" was the motto, as we can read on the embroidery that hangs on the wall. Here, Hansine's darning things remain at the ready, as though she was just out making some coffee.

"Magnusstua" is the name of the fine parlour. The door and window frames are formed in neo-Imperial style, as was the fashion towards the end of the last century, and the corner cupboard, the black rocking chair and the patterned sideboard are also typical of the time.

In the hall between the two rooms, two framed documents hang on the walls as visible proof of active public spirit: A diploma from "*Ny jord*" for clearing new land, and another from the National Society for Public Health, for good work in this field.

Fetching Water and Children at Play

The objects in the pantry and the entrance hall are perhaps those that best reveal the nature of women's work in the home. Here, we can follow the trail from the potato patch, via the potato masher, to hot, tasty potato cakes with butter that, in turn, has followed the path from the milking pale, via the separator, to the butter churn.

In the entrance hall, the yoke bears witness to many a strenuous trek carrying water to the house and the barn, and a soap whisk shows the younger visitor how one managed before detergents arrived in plastic bottles. In addition to these items, the house contains a wide variety of textile paraphernalia, including a spinning wheel, carding combs and a loom. Feminine diligence can also be seen in the embroidered tablecloths in the "Magnusstua" room.

The place of the children in the home can also be clearly seen on a visit to Skaftnes. The enormous child mortality rate is one of the sadder features of our none too distant past. A photograph from 1899 with grandfather Hans, parents and older brothers and sisters gathered around the open coffin of a small child who only reached the age of 2, can bring tears to the eyes of most of us.

On the other hand, we smile willingly, and perhaps in recognition, when we see what the children played with under the sloping attic ceiling. The upstairs bedrooms are also typical of their time, and include amongst other things, washstands and extendible beds. One of the rooms has been furnished as the "chamber maid's room" and here we find, amongst other things, a sewing machine and a wringer.

Every summer, Vestvågøy Museum arranges the Skaftnes Festival in cooperation with voluntary organisations on the island. At the festival, you will hear the blacksmith hammering away in his smithy, the spinning wheel whirring in the parlour, the jingle of loose change in the general store, and you will smell the aroma of freshly made coffee and waffles. Indeed, you can in fact smell this latter mentioned aroma throughout the entire summer season. But remember, lovely coffee and waffles are not the only reasons why you should treat yourself to a visit to Skaftnes.

Flakstad –
White Beaches and the Midnight Sun

lakstad smiles at you with its beaches white as chalk. Its pulse is the rhythmic beat of breakers rolling in from the great ocean. This tiny, green borough in the middle of the island realm of Lofoten consists of the island of Flakstadøy, and the northernmost tip of the island of Moskenesøy. Between these two islands is the narrow, fast-flowing Sundstraumen strait – an important communications artery in this land of boats.

Harbour Conditions in the Fishing Villages

There is a sense of history about traditional fishing villages like Sund and Nusfjord. With its antiquated architectural environment, Nusfjord was selected as pilot project during the European Preservation of Architecture Year in 1975. These two fishing villages face the Vestfjord, as does the abandoned fishing hamlet of Nesland. All three represent important aspects in the history of communications prior to the motorisation of the fishing fleet.

Fertile agricultural areas like those in Vareide, Flakstad and Fredvang, are situated on the island's outer coast. At present, the village of Ramberg is undergoing development and will become western Lofoten's most important outer coast harbour. The development of the harbours has greatly improved working conditions in fishing villages like Sund, Napp and Fredvang. In Mølnarodden and the surrounding district, the new industry – fish farming – has found a base.

Settlement in Flakstad is very scattered and includes many small, rural communities where traditionally, the combination of fishing and farming was the norm. Flakstad is the Lofoten borough where most of the population live on the outer coast of the island. Life there is lived beneath flaming, red skies and in a sea of mist.

Sund Fisheries Museum –
The Advent of the Motor Fishing Boat

FISKERIMUSÉET

A fog horn blows harsh and loud. A *Bolinder,* or was it a *Brunvoll,* drones away rhythmically. The shrill sound of hammer on anvil rings out. You have arrived in the realm of the audible. You have arrived at the Sund Fisheries Museum, which once, by way of a printing error, was described as the Sund Fixeries Museum – and perhaps that is what it should have been called, because the fixing of curiosities and peculiar objects is something that has always been characteristic of this museum, which incidentally was not established on the basis of project descriptions, planning documents and bureaucratic paragraphs.

This museum just simply developed, although not on its own.

A Museum is Born ...

Once upon a time – but not that long ago, only about 50 years as a matter of fact – a young, newly trained blacksmith set up a tiny smithy on an islet in the fishing village of Sund. Why did he do it? It was during the war, the fish-

There was a lot of power in a Brunvoll 50 hp semi-diesel. Hans himself demonstrates. (Photo: Helge A. Wold.)

ing boat owners had long since installed engines in their boats, but there was a shortage of goods – engines and other equipment were poorly maintained. Worn out *Heins* coughed and spluttered. Aboard the "Brottsjø" and the "Bølgen" *Bolinders* droned in dissatisfaction. In stormy weather out on the Vestfjord, *Wichmans* had problems, and winches got stuck. It was a long way to the shipyard here in the western Lofotens. The young blacksmith realised that there was work to be done here.

Things had to be repaired quickly so that the boats weren't stuck in dock when the cod were at their most abundant out on the fishing grounds. The blacksmith did not have much equipment himself, but in his imaginative way he ma-

"Ashlad and his faithful helper." Hans and Petra Gjertsen - two people who found, gathered and took care of things... They were awarded the Nordland County Culture Prize and the Flakstad Council's Culture Prize for their work. (Photo: Per H. Kirkesæther)

naged to fix most things. He welded, screwed and oiled – a true inventor, he became. A wizard, some said. But could a museum arise from this? Of course not. But by way of all the improvisation he employed to get things to work, the blacksmith developed a special interest in, and insight into, just about any technical, mechanical or simply just any moveable part. And great was his satisfaction when he finally managed to coax life into these moveable parts. He grew more and more interested in anything that hummed or whirred, ticked or tocked ...

Ashlad and his Faithful Helper

He was born in a fisherman's home "with one foot on the seashore" as he himself puts it. As a young lad he spent a great deal of time wandering along this shore. "I've found it, I've found it," he said, as did his close relative, Ashlad of Norwegian fairy tale fame. And he took care of what he found. He might easily find some use for a green glass float, a piece of rusty piping, or an old tin can. And as with Ashlad, before long, a faithful helper turned up. "She worked at the telegraph office and had a fixed income, so she bought me a welding set," the blacksmith once told me. And now they were two to find, obtain, and take care of ... For gradually the time came when the old drop-leaf tables were carted out the back door and replaced by Formica and teak tables. Chests and churns, wooden bowls, cod-liver oil funnels and lots of other "old junk" was thrown out of homes and boathouses and burned on bonfires. The small rowing boats rotted away on the shore.

Ashlad and his faithful helper took care of what came their way. But it was still no museum. In 1964, they came over an old, dilapidated "rorbu" cabin which they dismantled and moved to Sund. "The wages from the telegraph office were spent on nails," the blacksmith laughed. They crammed old domestic utensils into the cabin, together with tackle and ropes and "any old junk" as people used to say. The smithy was filled with tools and whirring bric-a-brac ... And that is how it became a museum. And that is how the fairy tail ended, or began ... Petra and Hans Gjertsen had begun to take care of part of our heritage ...

DERELICT FISHING VILLAGES – AND NEW ONES

The oldest boat engine in Sund dates back to 1907, the newest is from 1963. We are now going back to about 1905, when engines began to appear in the fishing boats, replacing the oars and sails. It is no exaggeration to say that the advent of the motor boat revolutionised the fishing industry in the course of a relatively short period of time. By way of his research, a historian named Jan Vea has provided a thorough analysis of structural and other changes that took place along the coast, verified by, amongst other things, some solid statistics. On the basis of his figures, Vea establishes the following fact: it was the fishermen from the Møre region who were the pioneers when it came to putting the new technology to use.

The fishermen of North Norway "sat on the fence" for a few years, until Troms became the pioneer county of the north. The motorisation process did not gain momentum in Nordland until 1914, but from then on things happened quickly – quickest in Vesterålen, slowest in the Helgeland and Salten regions. Yet as late as around 1920, half or so of the fishermen of Nordland did their fishing from aboard motor boats. On the seas of Lofoten, open boats with sails were still a common sight, especially among those from Helgeland and Salten.

Østre Nesland

Sund was, and still is, one of the major fishing villages in the western Lofotens, together with the time-honoured neighbouring village of Nusfjord. On your travels you should, however, make a detour to another type of fishing village: to the derelict, yet well-preserved fisherman-farmer's hamlet of Østre Nesland, which lies midway between its two "bigger brothers", Sund and Nusfjord. Østre Nesland evolved as a fishing hamlet in the 1850's. Imagine arriving in Østre Nesland on a winter's day in 1920-25. What would you see there? In the harbour, the fishing boats would be shoulder to shoulder, or drawn up on the shore if the weather were bad. You would see 15-20 "rorbu" cabins full of fishermen, most of whom came from Helgeland. And you would see a number of fish racks. You could drop into the general store and buy yourself a packet of Tiedemann's tobacco. The aroma of freshly baked bread would ooze out from the tiny bakery. The cod-liver oil factory on the hill would not smell quite as good.

Harbour Conditions and Development

Now, imagine that you return 30 years later. What do you see now? Perhaps there are a few open boats with outboard motors in the harbour. Only a few rorbu cabins remain. The fish racks are few and far between, and you can smell neither fresh baked bread nor cod-liver oil. What has happened during these 30 years? You will find the answer by looking out over the harbour. It faces the Vestfjord, open and unsheltered against the south-westerly storms. By no means a good harbour, but it was a short distance

from the fishing grounds and that was important when you were rowing out to find the cod. And should weather conditions in the harbour grow too bad, the small unmotorised boats of which there were still many around the year 1925, could be hauled up onto the beach. In 1950, however, the fishing fleet had long since been motorised, one or other open boat might still be found, but they all had outboard motors now. The harbour in Østre Nesland was not meant for motor boats.

The once vibrant and lively fishing village of Østre Nesland became derelict. It was the end of an era.

There are many derelict fishing villages along the coast of the Lofotens, but motorisation also led to the establishment of new fishing villages. A good example of this is Napp on the island of Flakstadøya. There is a good harbour there, but on the other hand, it was a long way to the fishing grounds when you had to row or sail there. With the advent of the motor boat, this disadvantage was eliminated, and Napp quickly developed into a modern fishing village.

Innovation Always Meets with Opposition

A fisherman came home from the slipway with his new engine. Inquisitive neighbours wanted to know how it worked. The owner told them it worked well, there was only one problem, "... it swallowed exhaust fumes." It turned out that the engine worked the wrong way round, taking in air via the exhaust, and expelling exhaust fumes through the air intake!! This story proves that knowledge of new technology was often lacking, and as is reasonable enough, the fishermen feared that they would not be able to cope with the problems. A touch of superstition might also be found at the root of their scepticism, expressed in such poignant remarks as "Engines are as great a disaster on board fishing boats as women, waffles and brown cheese ..."

Short-lived Opposition to Engines

The outermost part of the western Lofotens is characterised as a pioneer area with regard to the process of transition, and this applies in particular to Moskenes. This might seem something of a paradox because, as we have seen, the new technology aroused considerable scepticism and opposition here as in other places. The years prior to the First World War were characterised by intense yet short-lived opposition to engines. The fishermen claimed that the noisy engines frightened the fish away, that the motor boats would catch all the cod before they got to their spawning places, and that

the old Nordland-type boats were not constructed for engines. Protest meetings were held, and a ban on motor boats was demanded during the Lofoten fishery. Even the Lofoten Fishery Inspectorate were in doubt, worrying about disorder at sea and demanding that certain sea areas be reserved for fishing from rowing boats, a demand that was in fact implemented.

The Squire's Involvement

The squires, too, were sceptical. Jan Vea says that "they were largely on the side of the rowing boat fishermen." In 1908, the ageing squire of Reine asked Parliament to help limit the use of motor boats. It is not difficult to understand the squire's scepticism. The rowing boat fishermen were tied to one place, they came to the squire's village at the start of the season and stayed their until it was over. They hired rorbu cabins from the squire, bought their commodities in his shop, and they delivered their fish to him. A motor boat fisherman would be a mobile fisherman – and would consequently pose a threat to the monopoly of the squire. But despite the threats, it is nonetheless a fact that many of the squires here, outermost in the western Lofotens, were quick to acquire their own motor boats. When the aforementioned squire of Reine asked Parliament to limit the extent of these newfangl-

The fishing village of Sund with the fishing fleet in front of the Mansion. (Central Office of Historic Monuments' photo archives.)

ed operations in 1908, his sons and partners had already acquired two motor boats which were employed in gillnet fishing during the Lofoten fishery! And the squire of Nusfjord was to become a driving force during the process of transition.

A "Mobile" Fisherman?

How should one explain the squires' active involvement in a process of structural change that they clearly feared would deprive them of power and influence? Why did they voluntarily elect to dig their own graves? Let us dwell for a moment on the notion of the "mobile fisherman". How mobile was he in this first stage of transition? There were in fact several factors that limited his mobility. Firstly, the engines were small, and as late as 1920, the average engine could muster a mere 13 hp. Their speed was correspondingly low, and in favourable conditions, a sailing boat could go faster. Secondly, the motor boat fishermen were still dependent on having a rorbu cabin, both as overnight accommodation for the crew, and as a place of work for the land-based workers, i.e. those who baited longlines and repaired the nets. There was therefore no immediate risk that the squires might be subject to the mass migration of fishermen from village to village.

The danger of losing control was not imminent at such an early stage. The squires here have therefore probably chosen the short-term solution, as Jan Vea points out, deciding that they were best served by going along with the unavoidable development of progress instead of trying to fight it, thereby providing themselves with the opportunity of reaping profits as long as there was anything to reap from. The fact that fishing in the western Lofotens was exceedingly good during these early years was no doubt a contributing factor to the squires' decision.

The Poor Man's Dream of Owning a Motor Boat ...

In 1907, the three motor boats that were to be found here, on the outermost of the Lofotens islands, probably created quite a stir, and we can imagine that some cotter's lad or other, maybe taking part in his first Lofoten fishery, dreamed of some day owning his own motor boat. "Success" the boat would be called ... or maybe "The Trial" ... On second thoughts, he would name her after his mother, "Henrikka". And maybe this very same lad sat down at the kitchen table 10-15 years later to write an application to "The Sea Fishing Fund" for a loan to buy a motor boat. In that case he would soon learn that it was no easy matter.

The Fund was indeed established precisely to help poor fishermen of limited means, but a municipal guarantee for the loan was nonetheless required. At this point, the Mayor would be able to inform our fisherman that the Council required surety from "well-to-do guarantors." Sounds difficult. Maybe a bank loan would be easier? Our friend knew of a fellow who had got one, but he in turn said that the bank required guarantors, too, and that they also regarded the boat itself, and his house and home as security for the loan. Our young fisherman didn't even have a house or home. A few years ago, his neighbour had acquired an engine. He had been given credit by the motor manufacturer.

For Lack of a Rich Uncle

During the first years of motorisation, it was not unusual for the engine manufacturers, who were very eager to make a sale, to offer both ordinary loans and hire contracts on given terms. But these arrangements were short lived, and our friend was turned down. And since he had no rich uncles either, who might have served as guarantors, it all ended up with him standing in the squire's office one day, with cap in hand, begging for surety for the municipal guarantee and for a loan to cover the capital requirements that remained unmet, in order to fully finance the purchase.

Many a fisherman came to the squire's office on the same errand as our impoverished young friend. We have no record of how many, nor do we have any record of how many were turned away.

But various sources do show that many actually got what they were asking for. Often – very often – the squire would demand certain things in return for his goodwill. This might involve the fisherman being required to deliver his catch to the squire, or the far stricter demand that the squire be part-owner of the vessel. The latter condition was very common and meant that the squire could enjoy considerable control over operations.

Skipper on His Own Boat

The squire said yes to our fisherman, and after all the formalities had been dispensed with, he became skipper on his own fishing smack or cutter – one of the 140 motor boats to be found in Flakstad and Moskenes around the year 1920. And now he dreamed of how one day he would buy the squire's part, too, and become the independent, sole owner. Maybe he grew old before attaining his goal, or maybe he never actually got that far. Maybe, at worst, he lost his boat at a foreclosure during the inter-war years. During the recession and up until the mid 1930's, finding money to buy a boat became more and more difficult. The banks tightened up on the terms for loans. The State Fisherman's Bank, which succeeded the Sea Fishing Fund in 1919, provided loans that covered only 40% of total costs. For many fishermen, the dream of owning their own boat was never anything more than a dream.

But some of them sought new solutions, and now more and more fishermen joined together to invest in a shared vessel, usually in cooperation with one of the squires out here. This was particularly common in the westernmost parts of the region. It should also be mentioned that as early as 1915, a special boat insurance company was founded. The company gradually managed to build up such a stable financial base that towards the end of the 1920's, it was able to offer low interest mortgage loans for the purchase of new vessels or for the alteration of older ones. The fishermen of Moskenes made particularly good use of these initiatives.

"Nygaardsvold Boats"

In 1935 the Norwegian Labour Party came to power with Johan Nygaardsvold as prime minister. As part of the government's social profile, the state was to provide "crisis grants" for the purchase of fishing vessels. The condition was that only active fishermen who were members of cooperative societies were eligible for grants. There was little interest for this kind of financing in our region. Only a few state boats, or "Nygaardsvold boats" as they were often referred to, turned up in the western Lofotens. One might ask why. Perhaps the answer can be found in the terms of these loans, where the squire was excluded from owning any part of the boats as he was not an active fisherman. The cooperative philosophy never made the necessary breakthrough in this region, opposed as it was by the squires.

The years passed by. Courses for ship's engineers were held. The engines became bigger and more reliable. The boats became bigger, too, and one day the first boat with a wheelhouse showed up on the fishing grounds ... "A sheep shed," some laughed. It is said that once, under cover of night, some young pranksters in one of the fishing villages saw their chance to lay turf on the wheelhouse roof to emphasise the disgracefulness of "farmers at sea..."

People shared a wry smile, as they often do regarding anything new and unusual. Yet should a young lad on the post-war seas of Lofoten have caught sight of an open Nordland-type boat at sail – a highly unlikely event – he may well have thought, "It would have been fun to sail ... Granddad could do it."

Fishing boats need maintenance. Overhauling on the slipway in Sund. (Photo: To-Foto AS)

Storbåthallaren Cave

Five kilometres south of Napp, in rugged terrain, you will find a mighty, overhanging rock, a cave about 70 metres wide and 22 metres deep. The mouth of the cave is 9 metres tall, but at the back you have to crawl on your hands and knees. It is called Storbåthallaren and it is the oldest of the Stone Age settlements we know of in Lofoten and Vesterålen. The name, which means "big boat cave," comes from the fact that people used it as a winter storage place for the larger boats, or dories, right up until our own times.

Sensational Find

It was Lofoten's own "archaeological explorer", Kåre Ringstad, who found the Stone Age settlement in 1967. It was a very important find because for the first time, we were given a detailed insight into Stone Age life in the North.

Ringstad was on a boat trip with his family and had been fishing in the Nappstraumen strait when he decided it was time for coffee. They found a suitable place to land and after the coffee break, while Ringstad was looking around in his usual manner, he suddenly noticed an interesting overhanging rock. Upon taking a closer look, he walked right into the Stone Age settlement. On the way home his head was full of thoughts and his rucksack full of human bones. He hastily contacted Tromsø Museum. In the years between 1969 and 1971, excavations were carried out under the supervision of the archaeologist, Astrid Utne.

Life in the Cave

There is good shelter from the elements inside the cave, and thick layers of Stone Age human waste were found there. We can "read" almost 6000 years of exciting history from these layers of waste, from a time when sea level was about six metres higher than today. The objects found here included fishing tackle like hooks, harpoon points, and sinkers.

Other finds included spearheads and arrowheads, knives, axes and chisels made from slate, whetstones and grindstones. The tools were probably used to make tackle and boats, and for gathering fuel, hunting, fishing and carving. Bone needles (awls) and potshards from asbestos-based ceramics can provide us with details about work "indoors", about the sewing of clothes, tents and skin boats, and the preparation and preservation of food. Such finds show that Storbåthallaren Cave was not only a hunting station, but that people also lived here for longer periods of time. We can picture the extended family here: the men sitting sewing rough leather capes while the women were out checking the snares for birds, or off together hunting otters.

The Menu

The remains of the Stone Age people's meals bear witness to an exciting and varied menu, the Stone Age settlers ate a lot of fish and here the remains of bones from cod, ling, coley, halibut and tusk were found. Shellfish and sea snails were also on the menu. In the remains of their meals there were bones from no less than 16 species of animals and 37 species of birds, of which gulls and the now extinct great auk seemed to constitute the most popular dish. When it comes to mammals, the remains of seals, foxes, wild reindeer and otters were found. Surprisingly enough, the remnants of bones also tell of dinners consisting of forest animals like deer and beaver. And even more unexpected were the remains of cattle and smaller domestic animals like sheep or goats. No-one had expected to find that they kept domestic animals in Lofoten 3-4,000 years ago. No remains of vegetarian food were found, but this is because such remains decompose quickly – and most vegetables did in fact get eaten up! The extended family in the cave probably gathered berries, herbs and roots which they had for "dessert" or to spice their fish and meat with.

Battle Axe and Burial Finds

One of the finds of particular interest is the remains of a battle axe of the type that was in common use among cattle herders in southern and mid Scandinavia about 5,000 years ago. Did the Stone Age settlers use their battle axes for defensive purposes, or to attack? Burial finds from the Stone Age are very rare. In Storbåthallaren Cave, archaeologists found a woman's grave including a complete skeleton. They named the woman Olga. Human bones from various different individuals were found in several places in the cave. It is difficult to determine whether these burials have any connection with the Stone Age settlement, or whether the place was used as a burial ground at some later date.

Kåre Ringstad – archaeological discoverer. In 1963 he found the Stone Age settlement in Storbåthallaren Cave. His first major find.

Moskenesøy–
Magnificent Mountains and Maelstrom

The island of Moskenesøy is majestic. Man becomes insignificant in this rugged island countryside, where the Maelstrom – *Mosktraumen* – one of the world's strongest tidal currents, is next-door neighbour. The island is an eldorado for mountaineers and geologists. The mountains rise straight up from the sea, and at their feet a few, tiny fishing villages have managed to hang on. Traditional fishing villages like Hamnøy, Reine, Moskenes, Sørvågen, Tind and Å are all lined up along the inner coast of the island. The Lofoten Road comes to an end in Å. Along the shore of beautiful Reinefjord there are three tiny fjord hamlets with no road links, where the old combined fishing and farming traditions are still maintained.

From Mountainside Haymaking and Whaling, to Tourism?

There is not a lot of arable land in the borough of Moskenes, but haymaking on the steep slopes and mountainsides was common practice in the past, since most people kept domestic animals. Fishing has always been the major industry out here. The whaling organisation "High North Alliance" has its headquarters in Reine, the village with more whaling licenses than anywhere else in the country. Whaling has been going on here for generations. In more recent years, fish farming and tourism have become of increasing importance.

Up until about 1950, there were several small villages to the west of Å and around the Lofoten Headland. These villages were left derelict in 1951 though, after the first state grants had been awarded to encourage people to move away from the outer-coast villages of Hell and Refsvika.

Whaler in action: Brave heart, eyes front and a dog-end between his lips.

Cod and Communications

TELETEKNISKE SAMLINGER

The Norwegian Telecommunications Museum's Collection, Sørvågen

135 Years of Sørvågen Telegraph Station and Sørvågen Radio

We might well reflect in wonder at the fact that such a long, drawn out and craggy country as ours, on the outskirts of Europe, can offer telecommunications services to meet the highest of standards.

Many may indeed ask why Sørvågen, in the western Lofotens, set in Norway's perhaps wildest and most rugged landscape, was to become the scene where such extremely important chapters in the history of Norwegian and European telecommunications history were written.

Or might this inaccessible countryside itself provide the reason why Norway is today among the world leaders in the development of telecommunications ?
Sørvågen Telegraph Station and Sørvågen Radio have been very much in the limelight throughout the 150 years of our telecommunications history.

Why Lofoten – Why Sørvågen?

Every winter, fish worth millions of kroner were landed in Lofoten. The Lofoten fishery was one of the country's most important enterprises. It was believed that establishing telegraph and telephone services in Lofoten would lead to an increase in the country's income.
Therefore, the authorities invested in the development of telegraph lines in Lofoten, starting in 1860.
Wild mountains and ocean currents prevented the extension of the telegraph lines from Sørvågen, to Røst, Værøy and the Lofoten headland. The village of Sørvågen was therefore selected as the venue where several new inventions were to be tried out.

Norway's First Fisheries Telegraph Service – 1861

The year is 1859. Director General Motzfeldt of the post office wrote in his report from the Lofoten fishery that the yield would have been increased by 25% had telegraph lines been extended to the fishing villages. The Norwegian parliament – Stortinget – subsequently granted funds for a telegraph line to Lofoten. The Lofoten Line was completed in 1861, and its 170 kilometres of undersea cables and land lines comprised the country's first separate telegraph line that was independent of the main network. Nine fishing villages had now been connected to each other by telegraph lines during the Lofoten fishing season. These were Skrova, Brettesnes, Svolvær, Ørsvåg (moved to Kabelvåg in 1862), Henningsvær, Steine, Ballstad, Reine and Sørvågen. The stations were only open during the fishing season, from January to April. In 1868, the Lofoten Line was linked up to the main Norwegian network, and from 1873, Sørvågen Telegraph Station was open all year round.

This increased the yield of the Lofoten fishery for both the fishermen, the merchants and the state, while also creating many new jobs in the fishing villages. It was now possible to swiftly redirect the bait boats to where they were needed most, to transmit news about where the fishing was at its best, and to forecast stormy weather before it was too late.

Sørvågen Radio, 27.5.1930. (Photo: Wilse. Norwegian Folk Museum.)

Northern Europe's First Wireless Telegraph – 1906

"The mast was 50 metres tall. One of the workers climbed up and lay flat on his stomach across the top of it. I remember it well. We stood there with our hearts in our mouths," old Mrs. Hjørdis Lie from Sørvågen recalled.

We have moved on to 1903. On Lillehaugen hill in Sørvågen, a tall mast, comprising of several fir logs joined together and secured with 28 stays, had been raised. Similar masts had been set up on the islands of Værøy and Røst. The world's second permanent wireless telegraph station had been built for experimental operations. Would it be possible to telegraph across the dreaded Maelstrom without laying one single undersea cable?

Four years earlier, in 1899, Marconi of Italy had experimented with wireless telegraphy across the English Channel.

The fishermen and squires of the western Lofotens realised straight away what significance "the wireless" would have for them.

Elation in Røst – And a Long Way to Row

In 1902, Hermod Petersen, an engineer from the Telegraph Board, paid a visit to Sørvågen. He spent the night at squire Nils Arntzen's, assessed conditions, and left, convinced that it would be possible to establish a wireless connection between Værøy and Røst, and Sørvågen, that is to say, between the whole of Lofoten and the rest of the country. The Storting granted 15,000 kroner to the project.

The experiments carried out in 1903 provided results beyond all expectations. It is said that a man rowed all the way from Røst to Sørvågen, a stretch of 60 kilometres across perilous waters, to bring the good news: the signal from Sørvågen had passed over the Lofoten mountains, traversed the Maelstrom and been picked up in Røst.

On May 1, 1906, the wireless link between Sørvågen and Røst was officially opened – Northern Europe's first wireless telegraph. The Italians had got theirs the year before, but at least Sørvågen came in at second place in these worldwide statistics.

Storms and War – The Masts the Weakest Link

Even before the telegraph line had been officially opened, the masts had been damaged by stormy weather. The top of the Røst mast was blown down on February 6, 1906. On March 11 it broke again, and on April 11, the top of the mast at Sørvågen was blown down. Even the new iron mast raised at Sørvågen in 1914 was blown down in 1925.

During the Second World War, Sørvågen Radio became a very important link in the German communications network, and on

Boxing Day in 1941, the mast was demolished by British commandos during the raid on Lofoten.

Kaiser Wilhelm – Contact with Ships at Sea – 1908

"I remember Kaiser Wilhelm's

Postcard: "Sørvågen – Lofoten. Wireless Telegraph Station ." An important place of work for the women.

ship, the "Hohenzollern" was moored just off shore here. We kids were so excited. We climbed the hill and saw a little boat come to shore with a telegram," says Mrs. Hjørdis Lie.

The clerks at the telegraph office did everything within their power to provide the Kaiser with the best possible service, but it was all in vain.

Telegraph manager Øwre wrote the following in his telegram protocol:

July 15, 1906: "... have extra assistance today in connection with the German Kaiser's journey south ... do not disturb Sørvågen's possible coming correspondence with the ship."

July 16, 1906: "Heard a sign from the ship yesterday ... dispatched a number of telegrams ... the state of the network here, and the low mast made adjustments very difficult . I regret that this may provide an incorrect impression of both the equipment and those operating it."

July 12, 1907: "Called the "Hohenzollern" from 6 in the morning until 10.15 without being heard. We heard the ship call Sørvågen 10 times and Røst 4 times."

Sørvågen, then, did not manage to make contact with the Kaiser's ship. This was an embarrassment for the as yet young nation of Norway. However, not only did Kaiser Wilhelm launch the flow of German tourists to Lofoten, we can also thank him for the fact that the telegraph office in Sørvågen was opened for contact with ships at sea as early as on July 1, 1908, making it the first of its kind in Norway.

Increased Traffic

The telegraph office became more and more important to the fisheries. During the Lofoten fishing season in 1910, up to 500 telegrams a day might be dispatched here. There was, of course, considerably less traffic during the off-season.

The telegraph station in Sørvågen soon became too small, but in 1914, station manager Thorleif Johannesen was able to move with his family and all his equipment into the new and pleasant telegraph building, only a few hundred metres away from the old station.

Wireless Telephone to Hell and the Maelstrom – 1928

Norwegian Telecom obtained their first wireless telephone sets (radiotelephony) in 1919. The ordinary telephone lines now met with competition, just as the telegraph lines had been with the advent of wireless telegraphy.

Norway's first radio telephone station was also established in conjunction with Sørvågen Radio.

Lofotodden Radiotelephony Station at Hell began corresponding with Sørvågen in 1928. A few years later, Værøy also obtained a similar connection with Sørvågen.

Some important chapters in the history of telegraphy were indeed written in Sørvågen. It is sad that in 1976-77, the station had to be automated and Sørvågen Radio was closed down. The four telegraph buildings that had been in use from 1861 are still in relatively good condition, as is the 70 metre tall radio mast. The people in the west of Lofoten still appreciate the light emitted from it on dark autumn and winter nights.

The Sørvågen Telecommunications Collection will be opened in May 1996, as a division of the Norwegian Telecommunications Museum. The museum will provide a good impression of the development of telegraphy, telephony and radio in this country.

The museum is housed in the old telegraph station which dates back to 1914 and is situated just off the E10 highway.

The exhibitions will be closely linked to the following landmarks in the history of telecommunications in Lofoten and Norway:

- Norway's first fisheries telegraph service, the Lofoten Line, 1861
- Northern Europe's first permanent wireless telegraph service, 1906
- Norway's first permanent ship's telegraph, 1908
- Norway's first permanent wireless telephone (radiotelephone), 1928
- Norway's first permanent radio link, 1946

NORSK FISKEVÆRS-MUSEUM

Life in the Fishing Village

Today we'll go in through the back door, or "kitchen entrance" to the fishing villages. Really, we should have come in from the sea, because then we would have seen the fishing villages from their best side, since the buildings date back to the time when the sea was the "main road", the traffic artery.

Å – What a Place!

Å, in the year 1896. Life was not the same for the maid, Gjertine Hansdatter, and the squire's daughter, Ingrid, but both their lives were an integral part of "life in the fishing village." All of the 33 buildings in the fishing village of Å have their own place in the jigsaw puzzle. Here, we find the dwellings of the squire and those of the fisherman's family. In the rorbu cabins, visiting fishermen stayed during the Lofoten fishery. In the bakery, they baked the "daily bread". Food was stored safe and dry in the storehouse. There were animals in the stable and the chicken shed, animals that provided milk, eggs, meat and wool. In the barn fodder was kept for the animals. Here, too, you would find tools and vehicles like sleighs and wagons.

The outhouses and sheds contained various tools and tackle, and in the woodshed, a man would be in constant activity making firewood. In the nice, spacious boathouse, boats were hung up or lined up in rows. The blacksmith forged and repaired tools in his smithy for work both in the fisheries and on the farm. The shop sold goods of all kinds – food, clothing and tools. Warehouses, quays and a cod-liver oil factory were built so that fish could be landed and processed. Post and reception offices served to maintain contacts and help do business with the world outside the fishing village. A religious meeting house also belonged in the picture, as a popular belief in God also had its natural place with the people of the fishing village.

In order that worldly life might carry on, the people of Å had to utilise what nature had to offer: berries from the fields, fish from the lakes, and juicy, green fodder from the mountains. But most of all, life there was linked to the

Lofoten fishery and the riches of the sea.

Squires and Cotters

In 1896 there were two squire families in Å. There was the Nilsen family who were resident in Hennumgården House and the Ellingsens in that which is today known as the Mansion. They lived very close to each other, but that did not matter, because there was the best of relationships between the two families. The history of the squires is clearly visible in Å. It is more difficult to trace the history of the fishermen's families though, despite the fact that they constituted the majority of the inhabitants. According to the census of 1900, 94 people were living in Å at the time. Ten of them were of the squires' families. Eighteen were servants, of whom only one was employed by a fisherman's family. Three were in temporary employment with the Ellingsens and sixty-three of them constituted fisherman's families and cotters. The cotter's families did not own any land and had to rent that on which their houses stood, as well as hay-making lands and pastures, from the squire. Payment was made in the form of unpaid labour, usually performed during the summer haymaking season.

Squire Ellingsen had a large farm with two horses, ten cattle and several dozen sheep. In contrast, the domestic animals belonging to a fisherman's family usually included one cow and 5-6 winter-fed sheep. All the animals needed fodder and the hay for this was gathered in the Å-dalen valley and on the steep slopes overlooking the village of Å. Every tiny green patch was a valuable asset on the steep, rocky island of Moskenesøy.

Late Imperial Style and Standardised Houses

Both squires' residences were built in the 1860's and they dominate the scene in the fishing village. Considerable alterations were made to Ellingsen's mansion in the 1890's, turning it into an Imperial style building. In 1909, the house on Bekkhaugen hill was built – in three different styles: the Swiss and Jugend (German art nouveau) styles from Central Europe, in combination with the Nordic dragon style.

These houses provide a good impression of the relationship between the squire and the villagers. There were vast differences between people, both in wealth and power, not to mention in freedom of choice. The squire's children were the only ones who were sent away to get an education. The children from the fishermen's families normally did as their parents had done, they became fishermen and housewives. There is a cotter's house near the main museum building which was given a "face lift" in the 1950's.

The cottage shows how the average man and woman lived their everyday lives. After the Second World War, there was an increase in welfare. People wanted better living conditions than the small, crowded dwellings could provide, and the old houses were incorporated into "new", standardised houses. Traces of the old ones can still be seen in several places.

Public Image

The mansions of the squires constituted the public image of the fishing villages. At the homes of the better off, there were well-kept gardens with pavilions and exotic trees, shrubs and other plants. The Hennum garden in Å was renowned for this and was even mentioned in a weekly magazine as "a tiny piece of enchanting Eden." The mansion was often painted white, at least the walls facing the harbour were. It didn't matter too much about the back. That might lack panelling, and even be painted with the cheaper, red or ochre paint. White was the most expensive colour, and as such, it signified prosperity. This can be seen in the old, white-painted "Grandfather's house" in Å, where the bakery is today. Here, the back walls facing the storehouse are painted red.

The Squire's Family

There have been five generations of Ellingsens in Å, but it all started a long time before them. Let us begin with the merchant of Å, who's name was Maas. He had a foster daughter called Margrethe Sophie Kibsgaard (she died in 1881) who, in 1843 married the captain of a cargo vessel, Johan Ellingsen (1812 – 1900).

Margrethe gave birth to ten chil-

The village of Å, c.1900. The restoration of the Mansion has been completed and it now appears in the late Imperial style.
(The Norwegian Fishing Village Museum)

*C.P. Ellingsen and wife in 1895 on the steps in front of the Mansion
built by Johan Ellingsen in 1864. Ingrid is on the right.
(The Norwegian Fishing Village Museum, Å.)*

dren, but wealth had no power over sickness and death, and only three of the children actually grew up. The years between 1830 and 1880 were the Golden Age of the North Norwegian trading posts. Trade flourished, fish prices were good, and the fishing villages developed. In Å, development continued for several decades into the 1900's. This economic growth was closely linked to the fact that the fish merchants, like Squire Ellingsen, were given licences to export the fish that was ready for sale themselves.

The Year 1896

Margrethe and Johan's son, Christen Peder, or C.P. as he was known, took over the management of the family business in 1876. His wife, Henriette Mathilde from Trondheim, gave birth to seven children. Both husband and wife had their own areas of work within the business, which was called "Handelshuset Ellingsen, Å." C.P. was in charge of trade, including the purchase and export of fish, roes and cod-liver oil, shop-keeping, the shipping agency and the post office. Operations were kept running by workers like the clerk, the assistant manager, the baker, the blacksmith, the carpenters and the dockers. The lady of the house had an equal amount of work to supervise. She managed a large household with a governess, a babysitter, a cook, a housekeeper, several maids, a milk maid and farm hands. There were nearly always overnight guests on the estate because traditionally, the squire had also been the local innkeeper. During the Lofoten cod season, there were 40 ready made beds at the Ellingsens'. The farm was big, too, and the supervision of it required considerable effort from both of them. There were also farm hands and milk maids to take care of daily chores.

Winter and the Lofoten Fishery

Life has always been exhilarating and exciting during the winter fishery. The weather varies from frightful storms to the brightest sunny days with intense blue skies. The boats go back and forth to the fishing grounds, landing the catch on the quay. People shout and laugh and the gulls are beside themselves with all the titbits that are thrown into the sea. There is a pungency in the air, a mixture of tar and fish mingled with the tempting smell of freshly baked bread from the bakery. In 1896, no less than 32,280 hungry fishermen congregated in the fishing villages. The baker, who moved to Å during the fishing season, had plenty to do, since Å was a popular fishing station among a large number of these fishermen.

The Fishermen and Life in the Rorbu Cabin

The visiting fishermen in Å came largely from Beiarn and the Salten region. They came year af-

ter year and gradually became well acquainted with the local population and local conditions. The fishing villages were inundated with menfolk, and this meant that the girls were overtly coveted. During the autumn, the men checked their tackle and boats, and in mid January, they left their homes and set sail for Lofoten.

Ellingsen built many new rorbu cabins and in 1896 he had enough room to accommodate 300 men. Living conditions were cramped with 10-12 men, or two boat crews, in each cabin. Two or three grown men shared a single bunk. Everything was done in the main cabin room. Dripping wet clothing was hung up to dry, nets were mended and longlines baited, even their food was cooked here!

Fighting and antagonism? Oh yes, indeed there was– the men could get on each others' nerves, but as a rule there was a good feeling of solidarity among them. The fishermen spent their time and energy on a working day that began in the dark, around four or five in the morning. The start signal, a lantern or a flag, was hoisted at 6 a.m. The fishermen sailed or rowed as fast as they could out to the fishing grounds to compete for the best places to set their gear and haul in the catch. After a long day at sea, they gutted the catch ready for sale for hanging or salting. It was often late in the

Spring and the end of the season. The longlines are hung up to dry – ready for the next fishery in Lofoten or elsewhere along the coast. Photo taken in Sørvågen c. 1910. Northern Europe's first radiomast in the bakground. (Photo: Lind. Norwegian Folk Museum)

evening before they were back in their cabins.

The Lofoten Chest and Preparations

Fishermen's wives, maids, sisters and mothers along the coast of Norway from Finnmark to the West Country, spent the autumn months in preparation. The men and sons were to take part in the Lofoten fishery, staying away for several months. They needed to take a well-filled Lofoten Chest with them because the world's greatest cod fishery was also one of the world's toughest places of work. The women baked in September. The baking ladies went from house to house helping to bake griddle cakes and the wafer crispbread, or "flatbread," that kept so well. In October the domestic animals were slaughtered and then meat for the coming year was prepared. The meat was processed by either salting or drying. The best of the dried or salted meat was placed in the Lofoten Chests.

The Lofoten Chest was of vital importance to the fishermen. The women packed them with love, care and wisdom – to them it was a good investment ... A full grown man needed a lot of food and clothing in order to carry out hard, physical work during the coldest time of the year. Woollen clothing was vital along the coast. Coastal home crafts consisted largely of producing woollen clothing for the family – and for the menfolk in particular. Clothes made from the wool shed by the old sheep that were kept outdoors all year round, had the same effect as today's "Gore-Tex" garments, they were water resistant and when the woolly mittens finally did get wet, they still retained the warmth. For those working at sea, woollen clothing was therefore essential. The women spent as many working days getting everything together, as the men spent on the Lofoten fishery itself!

The Residents

The women in the fishing village didn't pack Lofoten Chests for themselves, but there was no shortage of work when it came to preparing food and woollen clothing. Their fields of work included the home, the barn and the men. They took care of everyone who needed food and care. In addition to this, they also took part in the fisheries, both before and after the catch was landed. They baited longlines, or tied the fish together in pairs at their tails, ready for hanging out to dry on the fish racks. During the Lofoten season, the women could earn money washing clothes for the crews of visiting boats. It was the squire who decided whether they should be allowed to let out lodgings to the fishermen, though. He had a monopoly on lodgings. If the weather was good, the women sometimes rowed out among the fishing boats and sold waffles and cakes to hungry fishermen!

The children, too, had to do their share of the work and took a great deal of responsibility in the home, looking after smaller brothers and sisters, fetching water and making food. Moreover, they also worked on the quayside, cutting out the cod tongues and threading the heads together ready for drying. Fish work provided them with cash, other work was rewarded with praise and acclamation from adults and satisfied parents.

The Age of the Open Boats

Å does not have a good natural harbour, but things worked well during the age of the open boat: Nordland-type boats of various, different sizes were moored in the tiny bay known as "Leira", in front of the boathouse. Here, you would find "fembøringer", "åttringer" , "firroringer" all the way down to the smallest "færingen", with its two compartments. The buyer boats – ketches and cargo vessels – came from afar to salt the fish. Steamers lay just off shore, selling bait to longliners. In 1896, motor boats were unheard of, people had only just got used to the steamers as carriers of heavy goods and travellers along the coast. In 1890, Å became permanent port of call for the steamer, and a local agency office was established. A new trend appeared in the villages with many of the visiting fishermen now arriving in Å on the steamer, or the "Local" as the boat was referred to – locally.

But then, as now, it was the catch that everybody was interested in: that was what they made their money from. Ingrid, the Squire's daughter, was 13 in 1896. She writes that there was excitement in the air: "All of us landlubbers stood around on the hilltops when the boats came in from the sea, waiting to see if they were lying low in the water." If the result was poor, everyone's spirits sank, and there was a dismal atmosphere in the fishing village. It was something else when all the boats returned heavily laden. Then there was "unusual vitality around all the quays and warehouses. People ran, shouted, laughed and waved their hands – the cod had arrived."

In 1896, the fishing was not particularly good. The total quantity of the catch ended up at 18,000,000 fish. The year before, in 1895, the result had been a phenomenal one, totalling 38,600,000. Still, fishing is unpredictable, exciting and stimulating. The dream of the great haul is ever present ...

June 12 – Fish Fetching Day

After Easter, the Lofoten fishery was usually over, the fishermen had returned home, and the hectic atmosphere was gone. The fish – "the money" – was left hanging on the fish racks until June 12, which was "fish-fetching day." Then, the jekt – this fabled North Norwegian cargo vessel – would be moored in the harbour, ready to do its part of the job. Towards the end of the 1800's it was the cargo ship "Lydia av Aa" that rocked across the Vestfjord with all sails set, bound for Bergen. She was loaded with fish, roes and cod-liver oil, all ready for shipping to the markets down in Europe. In exchange for the fish, the cargo vessel brought goods like flour, corn, salt, sugar, paraffin, tools and tackle to the north. Fish prices were therefore of the utmost importance to everyone. Many of the years of destitution in northern Norway were a result of poor fish prices and high corn prices. Coupled with a bad Lofoten season, these things spelled disaster.

The old cleric and poet, Petter Dass from Alstadhaug, put the situation into words:

If the cod us should fail,
what have we then,
What should we from here
to Bergen send?
The cargo vessels would sail
empty.

Cave Paintings in Refsvika

In the mid 1980's a group of archaeology students were in Refsvika working on an assignment for the Economic Maps Department. It was fine, summer weather and they were inside the 50 metre tall, 12 metre wide and 115 metre deep Refsvikhula Cave. There was great astonishment among those present when, in the light from the torches, red matchstick men appeared quite clearly on the walls of the cave.

Even the local inhabitants thought it strange that nobody had ever noticed the figures before. People had been living in Refsvika right up until the 1950's. They had often been in the cave, or *Kollhellaren* as they called it. The children used to play there, and if the weather was stormy during the summer, the cows would seek shelter there. Consequently, the women often sat, nice and dry, milking their cows in Kollhellaren Cave, yet nobody ever actually noticed the 21 red-painted matchstick men who are about 30-40 centimetres tall and can be found at three different places in the cave.

Where the Light Meets the Dark

The matchstick men were painted about 3,000 years ago with paint made from a red powder, probably from the iron oxide that can be found in the cave. They were painted where the cave branches off in three directions, in the darkest parts, where "life meets death". This might mean that the caves were used during ritual or religious activities. In mid-summer, the Midnight Sun fills the cave with a yellowish light. Could this have been the light by which the Stone Age people performed their rituals?

In the cave known as "Helvete" (Eng. = Hell) on the islet of Trenyken in Røst, similar painted figures have been found, and recently, 8 drawings of human forms were found in a large cave at Sanden in Værøy. Similar finds at several different places may be a sign of strong religious bonds in the area.

The cave paintings in the Refsvikhula Cave, or Kollhellaren, are the Borough of Moskenes' contribution to the ancient monument project "Footsteps in the north. A Guide to the History of North Norway and Namdalen."

The Maelstrom
– "Keep an Eye On the Current"

The Lofoten Headland's next-door neighbour is the Maelstrom – *Moskstraumen* – renowned as one of the world's strongest tidal currents in open waters. It flows between the island of *Moskenesøya* in the north, and some islets just north of the uninhabited island of Mosken in the south. The strait is about 4-5 kilometres across and 40-60 metres deep, and is considerably shallower than the surrounding sea. The tide fills up the Vestfjord twice a day, and the difference in height between high and low tides can be up to 4 metres. Midway between high and low tide, the current changes direction, and this is when the whirlpools begin to appear, with speeds of up to 6 knots.

Nothing else in Lofoten has been so prolifically described – and exaggerated upon – in so many languages. In 1539, Olaus Magnus' "Carta Marina" was published – complete with an illustration of a terrifying Maelstrom. In 1555, his work on the Nordic people's history came out in Rome. The Maelstrom is here described as an ocean vortex that runs up and down the sea every day, devouring great ships and spewing them up again! In 1591 the district bailiff wrote, " ... When the Maelstrom is at its peak, then you can see the sky and the sun through the waves and breakers,

Moskstraumen – the Great Maelstrom
Illustration from Olaus Magnus': History of the Nordic Peoples. 1555.

because they roll in as high as mountains." Similar impassioned descriptions of the Maelstrom can also be found in later accounts. The Norwegian clergyman and poet Petter Dass, the American author Edgar Allan Poe and the French author Jules Verne, are all in the same league. These authors describe the furious force of the Maelstrom, and Jules Verne also describes it as the world's most dangerous stretch of sea. They write of a current that howls, that rumbles like a buffalo herd on the prairie, that drags ships under, smashing them to smithereens against the sea bed. They describe great whales bellowing as they submit to the Maelstrom's vortices, while on land, the houses shudder at their foundations! The inhabitants of the outer coast villages of Hell and Refsvika lived nearest to the Maelstrom. They were annoyed at these exaggerations. They themselves had first and foremost treated the forces of the Maelstrom with respect – adapting their work and travels to it in a natural manner. Yet even so, it took its toll among the inhabitants.

Its ferocity was indeed a powerful experience. From the land, it was exciting and entertaining to watch, and the locals gladly climbed a fair way up the mountain-sides to get a better view of it. Today they say, "The Maelstrom, ah yes, that was our television when we were kids." Despite all the delirious descriptions of "the Great Maelstrom," the people of the outer coast regarded it as a gold mine – full of shoals of shiny fish.

An old Hamburger-map of the Maelstrom from 1683.

Værøy
– Bird Island in the Western Sea

Beautiful Værøy is the smallest of the boroughs of Lofoten. The mountains are characterised by gentle, protracting lines, lying there like a curved and inviting embankment, set in relief against the sea beyond. The inhabitants have settled for the most part in two villages – Nordland and Sørland – with 90% of them living in the village of Sørland. Owing to difficult harbour and communications conditions, one of the larger villages, Måstad, was abandoned after the war. The uninhabited mountain island of Mosken, out in the Maelstrom, belongs to the borough of Værøy.

"Worldly Assets"

The island's land-based "assets" are the great cliffside bird colonies, overlooking the sea, that were harvested for birds and eggs. The mountains and slopes are clad in green, nutritious rolling mountain grass. The major part of the island's arable land is to be found on its southern and eastern sides. Out here, surrounded by the sea, the sheep wandered free all year round. Today, there is not much agriculture on the island.

Eagle trapping is an incredible hunting tradition that the people of Værøy kept to themselves for a long time.

The fish in the sea have always been the islanders' "daily bread", and in 1930, 98% of the men on the island were fishermen. In the 1990's, over 80% of the work force is linked up to the fisheries. The new industries, fish farming and tourism, have also found their place in Værøy.

The abundance of eagles in Lofoten constituted a threat to sheep and lambs. At the turn of the century eagle trapping was therefore a common pastime among the young lads of Western Lofoten. At dusk during the late autumn, they caught the eagles with their bare hands, as seen above. This tradition was maintained in Værøy right up until the 1960's.

MÅSTAD

– A Museum in Its Own Right

Sheltered from the cold North winds, the houses creep close together against the sheer mountainside. An incredible place, Måstad, in the south west of the island of Værøy, faces the great ocean itself. And as the blue shadow of the mountains enshrouds the old buildings there, it is time to tell the story of the people of Måstad.

As with everywhere else along the coast, it was fish and the proximity to the best fishing grounds that formed the basis for settlement. But the people of Måstad had something else, something that made the people here seem better off than most. They had the mountains – and they had the birds. These were the greatest worldly assets of the people of Måstad.

The Mountains

With the exception of the sheer rock faces, the mountains of Måstad were for the most part clad in green. The innumerable flocks of birds fertilised the grass, making it juicy and nutritious. Here, the people of Måstad kept their "mountain sheep", that is, sheep that stayed outdoors both summer and winter. This far out to sea, the climate is mild and the winters are short with little snow.

The houses of Måstad hang on beneath the sheer mountainsides. Nearly 150 people lived on this sandy embankment during the inter-war years. (Photo: Dag Sørli)

The mountains where the "mountain sheep" wandered, were also the hayfields. Hardly anyone could have had more wretched and inaccessible hayfields. In many places they were so steep that the haymakers had to use ropes. And getting the hay back to the farm was a story in itself. Apparently, there has never been a horse on the island. The haymakers packed the hay in sacks that were thrown over the edge of the steep rock faces, tumbling uncontrollably down to the bottom, from where they were transported home in boats. Even though the sheep managed well enough in the mountains, the people still needed fodder for their cows. Most families had a cow, the better off had two, or even three.

The Birds and the People

The sheer cliffsides overlooking the very ocean itself are the realm of the seabirds, but they also comprised the pantry of the people of Måstad. In early May, the bigger gulls laid their eggs. By May 28, the kittiwakes would have laid their three greenish brown eggs, and before June 12, the fulmars, razorbills and guillemots would also have laid their large, single eggs on naked cliffside ledges.

The young lads and menfolk gathered the eggs. They most certainly constituted a supplement to existing provisions, yet the event itself was equally as much a sport to those taking part, and they competed in approaching the most difficult and inaccessible parts of the cliffs. Even so, there were few accidents. The people of Måstad knew the mountains, however, and for the most part they knew what they were doing.

The cliffside bird colonies were harvested three times. Then the young were left in peace. At home the women made pancakes with many eggs and little flour – you had to make savings where you could. When left buried in dry, fine sand, the eggs of the bigger birds could be kept well into the autumn, some even said right up until Christmas. Kittiwake eggs, however, had to be eaten while still fresh.

The people of Måstad also caught the birds themselves. No family in Måstad dared to meet the stormy, dark autumn and winter without at least one barrel of salted bird meat in the larder. Razorbills and guillemots were caught out at sea in nets. Cruelty to animals, many might say. And indeed, the Hunting Act of 1899 prohibited the catching of birds with nets, allowing peple to hunt on the cliffsides with a rifle instead. This particular law was, however, never observed by the people of Måstad. They claimed that shooting in the crowded seabird colonies, many lead to many birds inadvertently being wounded and inevitably left to die in pain. That was what the people of Måstad called cruelty to animals. In comparison, those who caught birds in nets always kept an eye on their gear, removing the birds at regular intervals. The birds' suffering was therefore short-lived, and those that were caught were put to good use. Man is meant to harvest nature, not over-exploit it. This was the maxim of the islanders.

Puffins were favourites on the Måstad people's menu. They were caught with the help of small dogs with pointed snouts that were kept solely for this purpose. The breed is known as *Lundehunder*, or puffin dogs, and in Værøy they are referred to locally as "Måstad" dogs because the breed only survived in the isolated hamlet of Måstad. They were an integral part of the pattern of life in the hamlet.

While hunting with nets was the work of the men, catching puffins with dogs was often the domain of the women and children, because when the time was right for this type of harvest, the menfolk were normally away fishing. So this part of the fisherman-farmer's work was also left to the women. The meat was the most important product, and the people of Måstad kept it for themselves. The feathers and down were the commodities that provided the islanders with a little extra money in their pockets.

The islanders never caught more birds than they could use themselves. They knew that the birds were a resource that had to be harvested with common sense.

"The people of Måstad with their farms beneath the wild mountains, their rocky shoreline and their Nordland-type boats. The authorities later built a good landing place and a track up the mountainside to Eidet, that the haymakers could walk along." (Text and photo: Carl Schøyen.)

Paradoxically, now that nobody harvests the seabird colonies anymore, the stocks have begun to decline.

The History of Måstad

There are not a lot of written sources concerning Måstad. Normally, we say that place names ending in *-stad*, can be associated with Viking times. The site of the old buildings at Eidet, not far from Måstad, has been dated back to 900 BC, and the cave paintings found at Sanden, opposite the hamlet of Måstad, have been dated 3,000 years back in time.

There are, however, many stories about Måstad. One of them tells of a King Mår who was said to have lived there. He had so many "mountain sheep" that by the time the first ones had arrived at the pen down on the farm, the last ones had not yet appeared on the ridge, 300 metres above the hamlet. An incredible story, yet more incredible is the fact that written sources confirm that the people of Måstad paid their taxes in the form of homespun woollen material. Måstad was the only fishing village in Norway where taxes were not paid in fish, as was the custom.

Moreover, tax accounts reveal that the people of Måstad paid just as much tax after the Black Death (c. 1350) as they had done

before. This might mean one of two things. Either the Black Death did not reach Måstad, or the land here was very valuable and therefore still in demand. The latter is the more feasible alternative.

The Sea

The sea was to become the cemetery for many of the inhabitants of Måstad. It was indeed the great provider, but the currents were strong, and there were treacherous shallows and rocks, and perilous gusts of falling wind from the mountainside. There were many shipwrecks, so many that by autumn, the people of Måstad would begin to wonder *who* would be lost at sea this coming winter, not *whether* anyone would be lost. A great majority of the shipwrecks occurred just off shore, and were sometimes so close that the villagers could stand by, powerless, and watch the tragedy unfold, without having any chance of going to the rescue. Both the Månesleia approach, and the islet of Månesodden, were infamous places where disaster often occurred.

The Dogs

The puffin dog is probably the Måstad people's greatest gift to posterity. The dogs are very small, rather like big cats. They are very agile, and have an extra toe compared to other breeds. The dogs creep into the screes where

"In Måstad every family had its own puffin dogs for the puffin hunt. And dogs and children played together between the houses. Sometimes they also climbed high into the mountains together."
(Text and photo: Carl Schøyen)

very similar to the dogs of Stone Age man, and must therefore be regarded as a kind of "primordial" dog. There are altogether 7 different breeds of Norwegian dogs. The puffin dog is the most unusual and the rarest of them. Today, there are no more than a good 600 puffin dogs left in Norway. All of them can trace their roots back to the tiny, isolated hamlet of Måstad.

Distemper

The history of the puffin dog is a dramatic one, and on several occasions the breed has been threatened with extinction. The first time was around the turn of the century, when a dog owner's tax of 8 kroner was introduced. That was an awful lot of money at the time, and therefore the dogs disappeared from most places except Måstad. In Værøy, it was accepted that the Måstad people could not make a living without their puffin dogs, and therefore, the tax was not imposed on the so-called "Måstad" dogs.

During the war in 1940-45, there was an outbreak of distemper in Måstad, wiping out the entire

the puffins nest, bringing the birds back with them. In many other places, puffins nest in burrows on grassy slopes. In Værøy, however, most puffins nest in the great rock-strewn slopes, or screes. This is why the dogs were so useful in Værøy, and the reason why the breed was maintained. The puffin dog is, for that matter, stock. Luckily, some puffin dogs had been taken into the care of Christie's Kennel in Hamar. After the war, five dogs were returned to Måstad. This proved to be just in time, because shortly afterwards, another outbreak of distemper wiped out all the dogs at the kennel in Hamar. The stock has been built up again from these five dogs, and now seems to be in good shape. Unfortunately, though, the black and white variety has been lost.

The puffin dog was essential to the way of life of the people of Måstad. The children were often given a dog each because, as we have seen, it was usually the women and children who hunted birds.

Bird hunting is not practised any more. Today's puffin dog is more a pet than a working dog. But then most of them are now only to be found in more urban districts down south. However, the shrill bark, shy disposition, vigilant attitude and unique body language of the "primordial" dog are still present in the puffin dog.

Moving Away

It is clear that the people of Måstad lived happily below their steep mountain cliffs – with no roads, no electricity and no harbour. They lived at one with a generous yet merciless Mother Nature. It was the lack of a good harbour that was to become the hamlet's bane. Previously, the boats had to be pulled up onto the stony beach, but with the advent of the motor boat in about 1910, this was no longer possible. The people of Måstad had to do their fishing from other parts of Værøy, where there were better harbour conditions. They were Værøy's first commuters. This went on for a few years, but then their families followed suit, leaving the hamlet behind for good.

From being a large, flourishing hamlet with up to 150 inhabitants and its own school, the hamlet of Måstad became more and more derelict, and in 1974, the last Måstad inhabitant left that rocky seaside embankment beneath the sheer cliffs.

It was the end of an era. As the blue mountain shadows enshroud the tiny houses that remain on the seaside embankment, we are in one way back at the beginning in the hamlet of Måstad – one of the most incredible outposts of northern Norway.

RØST
- A Gem on the "Edge of the World"

Originally, the word Røst comes from the old Norse word *Rost*, meaning whirlpool. The history of Røst is one of a people who have adapted to the forces of Nature, and have found their own lifestyle.

Røst is an exciting place with innumerable isles and islets – apparently as many as there are days in the year – and altogether distinctive natural surroundings. The inhabited islands are no more than 10 metres above sea level and settlement is concentrated on the pancake-flat area known as Røstlandet. The soil is rich, and for centuries, hundreds of sheep have grazed on the pastures amid kilometres of dry stone walls. The keeping of sheep provided important income for the inhabitants, and it still does.

Living with Nature, Living Off the Land

Off Røstlandet, the mountains rise, steep and monumental, straight upwards with the sea on all sides. They stand there all in a row, leading out towards Skomvær Lighthouse, at a suitable distance from man. About a quarter of Norway's total seabird stocks nest in these famous cliffside colonies. Man came out here, too, at regular intervals. He built hunting shelters and stayed here for some weeks at a time, harvesting the natural resources, the birds and their eggs. Birds provided a supplement to the basic means of subsistence – fish, and more fish. Today, Røst is one of Norway's most fisheries-dependent communities and is a major exporter of stockfish.

Those were the days ... Large bundles of puffins hang by everyone's door. (From the Røst Calendar, 1990.)

Of Pietro Querini and Natural Resources

"NAVIGARE NECESSE EST" – as they say in Latin. But navigation is difficult on a ship with no rudder or rigging, at large somewhere in the Bay of Biscay. The powers that be have let blow the great horns and all the floodgates of heaven have opened. Storm, real winter weather, as only we coastal folk know it.

The year is 1432. It is January. The Italian merchant, Pietro Querini had set out on what was supposed to be a peaceful trading expedition to Flanders, instead, he had become subject to the wrath of the gods. Now he and the rest of his crew are drifting helplessly about on the ocean, somewhere outside this world.

Great activity in Røst on a Spring day around 1910. Fish waste (guano) has been brought out on to the quay. Barrels of roes have been brought to the Gle-quay ready for shipping. The venerable old steamer, the "Hadsel" is moored at the quay ready for goods and passengers. (From the Røst Calendar, 1982.)

"As yet, the world had still not become round," and one might easily fall off.

After weeks in an open lifeboat, where death was a daily guest, the few remaining survivors finally made land on Sandøy, outermost of the islands of Røst. After further weeks of fighting against hunger and cold, the crew were finally found by the "natives".

A Valuable Account

We can understand that Querini, who had been closer to death than to life, bowed down in homage to his saviours, and their simple way of life. Upon his safe return to Venice, he was wise enough, our good Pietro, to make a written account of his journey. Querini's account is an historic document of great value and significance to North Norwegians. It is the first one to describe everyday life, not only in Røst, but also for the rest of North Norway.

He writes kindly of the people of Røst – the men who saved him, and the women. He hails their simple way of life, their diligence and abilities, and their piety. Not with one single breath does he imply that he would rather have seen better days among his own kind, living it up in Venice, dancing to the delicate sound of the harpsichord, drinking from crystal glasses full of sparkling wine, entertaining gold-adorned ladies with soft complexions ...

Indeed no. A nobleman bows his head, steps into the fisherman's earthen hut and sits down at his table. Fish, meat, bread and milk – filling, nourishing food for hard-workers, unfamiliar tastes to the noble palate. Our good Querini is noble enough so as not to exalt himself. He joins in the simple life of the islanders. He "degrades" himself to cleaner – swinging the broom for his hostess.

The First Italian Stockfish Importer

In May 1432, came the day when the surviving Italians could return home to Italy. Querini may have become the first stockfish importer, since it was stockfish he brought with him as provisions for the journey when he left the island. He writes, "... on behalf of the woman, he presented me, as being of superior in rank to the others, with sixty stockfish dried in the wind, and three large loaves of rye bread, as round as we were."

Pietro Querini was not forgotten. His fantastic story lived on in oral traditions through the centuries to follow. Although 500 years were to pass before his own people from the warm beaches of the Mediterranean were to visit our homely shores. In 1932, a stone monument was raised on the island of Sandøya, in memory of the unfortunate nobleman.

Prominent guests from Italy once again found their way to Røst, and the Mayor of Røst was man enough to make a speech – in Italian, of course.

"The Fish in the Sea are our Daily Bread ..." sang Petter Dass. And he was quite right. For the people of Røst the old ties to Italy have been very important. In more recent times, the Mayors of Røst have been invited to Italy as special guests. It's all about stockfish. Stockfish and Catholicism! Because, in the final analysis, it is the righteous Catholic who makes it possible to live out in Røst. During the Catholic season of Lent, stockfish goes like hot cakes in Italy. Not only does the stockfish they eat come from Norway, but as much as 30% of Norwegian stockfish exports come from Røst alone.

Is there any wonder that we maintain and cultivate our Røst-Italian connections?

Bird and Fish

Most outsiders who find their way to Røst have one main interest – bird watching. Every year ornithologists visit Skomvær and the other islands to examine the stocks. Perhaps you will find the world's most famous seabird colonies here – Vedøya, Strofjellet and Nykene.

Today, the sea and the birds rule on Skomvær and the other islands, but people have also lived out there – in the middle of this rather sizeable pantry. The relationship between the people of Røst and the birds, you see, does not only involve binoculars and statistics – the local inhabitants also have long-standing traditions in the harvesting of birds – for meat and eggs. Birds have been an important supplementary source of food for centuries, and many traces of this can still be found.

There had probably been landed estates out on Storfjellet – Sand and Husan –since the 1200's. The homesteads are of a design which has not been found anywhere else in Norway. You have to go all the way to the old settlements in Iceland or Greenland to find such architectural traditions. In addition to this, the remains of lesser buildings can be found round about on the islands. These are often the remains of hunting lodges that were used during fishing, bird trapping, egg gathering and hay-making.

A Successful Combination

The struggle for existence has been a hard one out among the islets and skerries. So man adapted himself to Mother Nature's own order, in the hope of wringing from her his meagre way of life. In April, the men often moved "westwards", out to the bird colonies to catch birds. The women and children remained at home and took care of the domestic animals, and the household chores. At this time of the year, the fish might also be in the west, by the bird colonies. This provided a successful combination that guaranteed food for hungry stomachs throughout the dark autumn months – and saved thousands of oar strokes since the distance to the fishing grounds might thus be halved.

May was the month of eggs. Seabird eggs from the islands were in such demand, that the men didn't mind risking life and limb hanging on a rope in the middle of the cliff face to get hold of them! What did not end

The islanders treated the seabird colonies as their pantry, fetching meat and eggs from the steep cliffs. Here are four satisfied egg collectors at Vedøya in Røst, 1956. (Poto: Sven Hörnell)

up in their own stomachs was easily marketable merchandise on the mainland and might be exchanged for wood to build boats, or to use as firewood. Such things, the people of Røst had to barter for elsewhere. The wealth of the islanders was to be found in eggs, salted bird meat and salted fish – but not so much in hard cash.

After the hay-making had been done on sparse home soil, the mountain islands had to be put to the sickle. The birds had been the origin of all the fertiliser that nourished the juicy mountain grass, thus providing an essential supplement towards keeping the cows and sheep with winter fodder. Neither mowing machine nor tractor were any use here, only raw manpower and female get-up-and-go.

A Lifestyle in the Blood

Throughout the generations, this constant rotation of tasks became something more than a perpetual struggle against hunger and the elements – it became a lifestyle that was "in the blood." Ask an old man about bird hunting or the perilous gathering of eggs, about days on end at the oars and arduous hay-making, and he will hardly mention the gruelling toil of it all. This was *life* itself.

Quotes from Querini's Own Account

"Their homes are round and built of wood, with nothing but an opening for light in the middle of the arching roof. During the winter, it is so unbearably cold that they cover the opening with fish skins that have been treated in such a way as to let a good deal of light seep through. They use thick woollens from London and other places, and do not use skins much at all. In order to get their children used to the cold and make them better able to tolerate it, they take their new-born babies when they are four days old and lay them naked beneath the opening, removing the fish skin and letting the snow fall on them."

"In the spring innumerable wild geese came and built their nests on the island, many of them close to the houses. They were so tame from never being frightened there, that they simply got up and let the women calmly take what eggs they wanted – eggs from which the women made omelettes for us. When they left, the geese came back to the nest, sat down to brood and were not frightened by anything else. We found this quite astounding, along with a lot of other things that it would take too long to go into." (*From Helge A. Wold: "I Paradisets første krets"*)

BiRd Life in Lofoten

There are lots of birds in Lofoten. Birds from the lakes, the shore, the marshlands, the sea, the mountains and the moors all meet on the archipelago. Two hundred and fifteen different species have been recorded on the island of Røst, and the list is ever increasing. In an island realm like Lofoten, however, it is the ducks, waders and sea birds that dominate. The most common ducks here include mallards, mergansers and eider ducks, the latter being known as "ea" in the Lofoten dialect. Eider ducks were highly cherished here, because of their eggs and down. Among the waders to be found along the shore and in the marshes we might mention oystercatchers and curlews.

Over a million birds nest in the cliffside colonies of Røst – Hernyken, Trenyken, Vedøya and Storfjellet, and in the Mostadfjellet mountains in Værøy.

There is hustle and bustle and a deafening racket here during the nesting season. The rocky, mountain faces are "fully booked" from top to toe by discerning birds who know exactly where they want to stay, whether it be in the penthouse, or down by the sea. There are kittiwakes, black backs, razorbills and guillemots, puffins, black guillemots and cormorants. But, after the puffins, it is the gulls that are the "national birds" of Lofoten. They dominate by their very presence, and there are several species including black backs, kittiwakes, common gulls and herring gulls.

On the steepest mountain walls, the proud sea eagles nest. The species is now on the increase after a period of stagnation. Only a few decades ago, the people of Værøy caught and killed sea eagles with their bare hands from special eagle trapping hides.

Illustrations from the book "Fugler på Røst" (The Birds of Røst – also available in English)
by Steve Baines and Tycho Anker-Nilsen.

Of Atmosphere, Weather and Humour

To be sure, it can be trying when the north wind blows with a vengeance. There are moments when you think "I wish I were in a warmer country," while the autumn and winter storms vent their wild and unrestrained rage on people and buildings. Salty sea water and sand are tossed over the village and road, drying in white, salty stripes – unless the rain washes them away. Perhaps you had washed your windows the day before, before you heard the weather forecast ... Thank heavens for the Met., for the fact that we are indoors, and that none of the boats is out at sea! They stay in land on a day like this. By the way – did we shut all the windows? And what about that pile of planks near the grocer's, have they been properly secured? The storm rages day and night. There are power cuts. Chaos and darkness. A flash of light outside the window, a deep rumbling can be heard. The telephone rings, we answer "No, don't worry, we are certainly not going out!" The storm has torn off the neighbour's roof, and corrugated iron sheets are flying all over the place. Dangerous? Exciting? Scary? Fun? The answer is: Yes!

As soon as it calms down, you seem to laugh and everyone gets a word in at the local shop – about Borgny and Jens' caravan that was lifted up into the air and smashed into Liv's new gateposts! Or Arne's veranda that the wind hurled into the sea. "Never! What do you want a veranda for in this weather? " As long as no lives are lost in the storm, sardonic humour is the best medicine. At least there is plenty to talk about here, where the weather is of such great significance.

All memories of the bad weather vanish completely as soon as the calm has settled over the bay. The fishing villages stand there, mirroring themselves off the quayside, whether in the sharp, bright sunny days of March, or the deep red August sunshine.

"There's no place like home," we say, knowing that the generations before us said exactly the same thing, just as overtly happy.

From Land of Fables and Fantasy...

to Modern Tourist Attraction

– A Historical Perspective on Travel in Lofoten –

For thousands of years, the natural surroundings and culture of North Norway and Lofoten have attracted the attention of outsiders – both from the south of Norway and from the rest of Europe. Even as far back as two thousand years ago, the Greek historian, Pytheas, wrote an account of this strange land in the north, with its light nights and its perilous Maelstrom.

The Midnight Sun, troll-like mountain formations and exotic culture formed a basis for fables, fantasies and myths about our region and the people who lived up here.

A wealth of natural resources like fish, furs, skins, walrus tusks (the ivory of the time), and eider down attracted seafarers, merchants and pirates.

Explorers and scientists acquired new knowledge of the region, thus contributing towards the opening up of the north. In 1553, Englishman Richard Chancellor made Knyskanes into an attraction by renaming it the North Cape, while an Italian monk and scientist, Francesco Negri, unveiled the myth of the Great Maelstrom in 1764. And the latter, being the first "North Cape tourist," also aroused interest in the phenomenon of the North Cape by uttering the following words, "Here I am at the North Cape. On the edge of Finnmark, and I might say on the very edge of the world, since there are no inhabited lands further north. My curiosity has now been satisfied, and I can return to Denmark, and, God willing, to my own native country."

Royal and princely travellers also made considerable contributions towards stimulating interest in the northern coasts. Our Danish-Norwegian king, Christian IV rounded the infamous Maelstrom in 1599, sailing on northwards to drive Dutchmen, Englishmen and Russians from Norway's northern coast, while simultaneously putting an end to the most notorious pirate of the time, Jan Mendoza.

In 1795, the French crown prince, Louis Phillipe, fled from the Revolution and made North Norway famous in his home country with the help of his visits to Lofoten and the North Cape. Our own Swedish-Danish king, Oscar II, created an interest in trips to the north by way of his journey to the North Cape, in which Lofoten was also on the itinerary.

However, the northern regions, including Lofoten, were probably marketed most efficiently by Kaiser Wilhelm, this friend of Norway who visited our coast many times around the turn of the century and climbed many a mountain, in Lofoten, too – from Mount Digermulkollen in the east to Mount Hellsegga in the west.

Chronicles from journeys north, with varying degrees of credibility, have often created impressions of North Norway as a strange land "far north of civility." Let us consider some of the conceptions of our region that have appeared through the ages:

There were many ancient myths about the northern regions. There were one-legged people here, and people with dog's heads, or horns

Kaiser Wilhelm and travel companions on Mount Digermulkollen in 1889. The Kaiser is in the centre.
From "Kaiser Wilhelm's II Reisen nach ..." Paul Güssfeldt, Berlin 1890.

on their foreheads. In the year 1070, Adam of Bremen mentions that Amazons lived up here. Myths of a more pleasant nature tell us of the "hyperboreans", a positive people, one of whom was the mother of the Greek God, Apollo. From the Viking Age, we hear of Lapps, well-versed in the art of sorcery, and of beautiful yet wicked women with power over men.

After the Black Death, the northern regions fade into oblivion. The countryside and people of the province are not mentioned again until 1432, when an Italian, Pietro Querini, and his crew drifted ashore in Lofoten. They provided an admirable impression of the people of Røst – as those "in the first circles of Paradise" – a skilful, god-fearing, honest and innocent people. In 1512, however, the Archbishop of Nidaros described the region as a frozen land full of monsters.

In his book *"History of the Nordic Peoples"* written in 1555, another man of the cloth, the Swedish prelate Olaus Magnus, presents a mixture of fact and fable. In 1591, bailiff Erik Hanssen Schjønnebøl, who was married to a North Norwegian, provides an interesting and more plausible account of Lofoten and Vesterålen.

As we can see, impressions of the northern regions changed frequently. During the first decades of the 1800's, the concept of the idyllic, as opposed to the magnificent, was fostered. In 1827, district governor of Drammen, Gustav Petter Blom, described Lofoten as follows:

"Lofoten is as lacking in natural beauty as can possibly be imagined ...As ugly as the eastern coast of Lofoten is, it is yet surpassed in sheer rawness by the western coast ... and ugliest of all is Sund in western Lofoten."

So what about the Lofoteners' self-esteem after such a broadside? Was there any hope?
Indeed there was. The years passed and attitudes changed.
Romanticism came to the rescue. The cherished authors Bjørnson and Lie altered the Norwegian impression of North Norway. In 1869, Bjørnson writes that Lofoten in particular is the highlight of the north – "a drama at sea," while Lie recreates the myth of the northerner's well-developed imagination. In 1912, Carl Schøyen's classic work *"Nord i være"* – Up North in the Fishing Villages – was published. He was the northerner's own poet and the book is full of respect for the region and the people of Lofoten.

A variety of travelogues describe the northern regions. North Norway, and Lofoten in particular, has come into fashion – a trend that will last for over 100 years. New, improved communications – beginning notably with the Coastal Steamer a hundred years ago – coupled with intensive marketing, have made it possible, and desirable, for more and more people to visit this "remarkable and distant land." Our number one holiday attraction, rorbu cabin tourism, began on a small scale towards the end of the 1930's.

Today, tourism has become one of Lofoten's most important industries and offers a complete set of rewarding and varied sights, attractions and activities. In recent years, this has led to an almost explosive increase in tourism in Lofoten.

Lofoten's countryside and culture are attractive, but vulnerable.

North Norwegian countryside, culture and character are constantly sought out by travellers from other parts of the world – now, as they were a hundred years ago. So far, Lofoten has profited from tourism. But if this success is to continue, tourism must be based on the sustainable use of the local natural surroundings, culture and human resources.

The people of Lofoten want to maintain control of developments. We want to limit damage to the countryside from wear and tear, to solve traffic problems, and to take care of architectural traditions and the place of the fisheries and agriculture in relation to the development of tourism.

We need help to do so, including that of the guests who visit our island communities.

Tourist Information Centres in Lofoten

Svolvær	Tel. 76 07 30 00
Stamsund	Tel. 76 08 97 92
Leknes	Tel. 76 06 05 94
Ramberg	Tel. 76 09 34 50
Moskenes	Tel. 76 09 15 99
Værøy	Tel. 76 09 52 10
Røst	Tel. 76 09 64 11

Bibliography

Ackermann, Asbjørn: "Skolehistorisk stoff fra Vestvågøy ved århundreskiftet", Lofotr, Årbok for Vestvågøy historielag, 1989.
Aftenposten 18.mai 1995.
Austrem, Liv Marie og Guri Ingebrigtsen: Feskarbonden og andre kvinnfolk. Orkana forlag. Stamsund 1992.

Baines, Steve og Tycho Anker-Nilssen: Fugler på Røst. Utgitt av Røst kommune, u.å.
Balsvik, Randi Rønning: "Kvinner i nordnorske kystsamfunn", i Historisk Tidsskrift, nr. 4 1991.
Berg, Per: Hol bygdebok, Bodø 1971
Bergsland, Knut og Magga, Lajla Mattson: Sydsamisk-norsk ordbok. Oslo/Kautokeino. 1993.
Bertelsen, Reidar /Tone Rørtveit: Om Vågan. Den første byen i Nord-Norge.
Bertelsen, Reidar: Er Vardø og Hammerfest de eldste byene i Nord-Norge? I Håløygminne nr. 2 1990
Bertelsen, Reidar: Lofoten og Vesterålens historie. Fra den eldste tida til ca. 1500 e. Kr. Utgitt av kommunene i Lofoten og Vesterålen. 1985.
Bjørgo, Narve: "Vågastemne i mellomalderen" I: Hamarspor, eit festskrift til Lars Hamre. Universitetsforlaget 1982.
Bjørnstad, Hans J.: Av Lofotfiskerens saga. Myten på nært hold. Gyldendal Norsk Forlag, Oslo 1970.
Blix, Dagmar: Gamle Lofoten. Rune Forlag, Trondheim 1975.
Bottolfsen, Øystein: "Lub og undermåls italiener", Lofot-boka. 1984. Værøy.
Brun, Håkon: Middelalderbrev fra Vågan. Årbok for Vågan 1989.
Brun, Håkon: Vågan i sagatekstene. Årbok for Vågan 1990.
"Bygdeavis for Moskenes", sommernummer 1982

Collinder, Bjørn: Ordbok till Sveriges lapska ortnamn. 1964.

Dass, Petter: "Nordlands Trompet", i Hegglund, Kjell og Sverre Inge Apenes (red.): Samlede Verker 1 - Nordlands Trom-pet. Gyldendal Norsk Forlag. Oslo 1980.
Diplomatarium Norvegicum bd. I - IV. Christiania (Oslo) 1847-1972
Diverse små publikasjoner/brosjyrer om Lofoten.
Drivenes, Einar-Arne, Marit Anne Hauan og Helge Wold (red.): Nord-norsk kulturhistorie bd. 1-2. Gyldendal norsk forlag. Oslo 1994.

Edvardsen, Edmund: Den gjenstridige almue. Skole og levebrød i et nordnorsk kystsamfunn ca. 1850-1900, Oslo 1992
Elstad, Kåre: Eit storbryllup i Vågan på 1300-talet. Årbok for Vågan 1990.

Grundstrøm, Harald: Lulelapsk ordbok. Uppsala 1946-1954.
Grøt-tland, Kristine Lind: Daglig brød og daglig dont. Fra nordnorsk husstell og hjemmeliv. Oslo 1962.

Helland, Amund: Topografisk-statistisk Beskrivelse over Nordlands amt. Aschehoug

& Co., Kristiania 1907.
Helnes, Johan: "Den gamle skolestua", Lofotr, Årbok for Vestvågøy historielag, 1985.
Herschend, F.: The origin of the Hall in Southern Scandi-navia. Tor, 25, Uppsala. 1993.
Håkon Håkonssons saga. Aschehoug 1964.

Jenssen, Frank A: Boka om Lofotfisket. Forlaget Nord. 1984.
Jenssen, Frank A: Lofoten. Lopo media forlag AS. 1994.
Johansen O.S. & Gerd Stamsø Munch: Borg in Lofoten - an interScandinavian research project. Norwegian archaeological review 21/2. Oslo 1988.
Johansen, Nils: "Fra Valberget skole i gamle dager, Lofotr, Årbok for Vestvågøy historielag, 1989.
Johansen, O.S.: Viking Age Farms: Estimating the Number and Population Size. A case study from Vestvågøy, North Norway. Norwegian archaeological review 15/1-2. Oslo 1982.

Klepp, Asbjørn: Nordlandsbåter og båter fra Trøndelag. Grøn-dahl & søn forlag a.s. Oslo 1983.
Knutsen, Nils Magne (red.): Nessekongene. De store handelsdynastiene i Nord-Norge. Gyldendal Norsk Forlag. Oslo 1988.
Korhonen, Olavi: Svensk lulesamisk ordbok. Umeå 1979.
Kristiansen, Kaare: "Lærer og altmuligmann O.J. Lauvdal", Lofotr, Årbok for Vestvågøy historielag, 1991

Langs vei og lei - Samferdsel i Nordland (s.513) ISBN:82-7416-021-5
Leonardsen, Leif: "Fra min egen skoletid", Lofotr, Årbok for Vestvågøy historielag, 1989.
Lindbekk, Kari: Lofoten og Vesterålens historie 1500-1700. Det lå muligheter i strevet. Utgitt av kommunene i Lofoten og Vetsrålen. 1985.
Lofotboka 1980 (s 68-75). ISBN: 82-90030-51-7
Lofotr, Årbok for Vestvågøy historielag.

Mathiesen, K.O.: Handelshuset Ellingsen, Å. 1843-1943. Tradisjon og historie. Fabritius & sønner. 1943.
Munch, G. S.: Høvdinggården "Borg i Lofoten". Ottar 4/187. Tromsø 1991.
Myrvang, Finn: "Samiske kuturspor i nordlandske stad-namn" i rapporten Stadnamn og kulturlandskapet. Helleland, Botolv og Margit Harsson (red.). Avdeling for namnegransking. Universitetet i Oslo 1995.
Myrvang, Finn: Nøkkelen til Utrøst. Stadnamnprosjektet i Nordland. Lofotboka forlag, Værøy.

Niemi, Einar m.fl. (red.): Trekk fra Nordnorges historie. Gyldendal norsk forlag. 1978.
Nilsskog, Audun: "Ein skolemorgon i mørketida", dikt, Nordnorsk dikting bd.2, Bodø 1983

OTTAR, populærhistorisk tidsskrift utgitt av Tromsø museum Diverse hefter.

Posti, Per: Gunnar Berg 1863-1893. Minneutstilling 1993. Katalog. Tromsø kunstforening/ Ateliér Lofoten. 1993.

Radiotelegrafi til bruk for den høiere undervisning i telegrafvæsenet, Kristiania 1913 (s 1 - 145).
Ryvarden, Leif: Lofoten og Vesterålen. Reise og kulturguide. Nortrabooks 1991.
Ryvarden, Leif: Lofoten og Vesterålen. Universitetsforlaget. 1981.
Røde, Gro: På et berg eg kalla mett. Hverdagsliv og fraflytting. Lofotodden 1900-1950. Orkana forlag. 1994.

Schiøtz, Ottar: Fra årer og segl til motor. Om motoriseringen av fiskeflåten i Moskenes og Flakstad. Lofoten fartøyassuranseforening. 1915-1985. Lofotboka Værøy. u.å.
Schønnebøl, Erik H.: Lofodens og Vestraalens Beskriffuelse 1591. Gjenopptrykket i Kari Lindbekk: Lofotens og Vesterålens historie bd. 2 1500-1700
Selnes, Leiv: "Lærar og kjerkesongar Eidhammer", Lofotr, Årbok for Vestvågøy historielag, 1989.
Sletteng, Kjell: "Åpninga av Vestvågøy museums nye avdeling i Skaftnes", Lofotr, Årbok for Vestvågøy historielag, 1992
Småskjær, Svein: Lofotbilder 1. Vågan 1867-1910. Småskjær i samarbeid med Vågan historielag. Forlaget Arctandria 1987.
Sneve, Arnt og Kjell Sandvik: Lofoten. Cappelen forlag. 1974.
Snorres kongesagaer. Gyldendal 1979.
Soga um Grette Asmunsson. Det norske samlaget 1912.
Solberg, Bjørn m.fl. (red.): Lofoten - I går - idag - i mor-gen, bd. 1-2-3-4, 1975.
Steinsland, G: De norrøne gullblekk med parmotiv og norrøn fyrsteideologi. Collegium Medivale 1990/1.
Storeide, Mareno: Fra lofotkokkens gryter. Orkana forlag. 1994.
Storeide, Vebjørn: Vestvågøy, midt i Lofoten. Orkana forlag, 1994.
Svendsen, Reinert: Historiske efterretninger om Værøy og Røst. I kommisjon hos Aschehoug & Co. 1916.
Sæter, Oddrun: Kunstnerkår i nord. Kommuneforlaget. Oslo 1989.
Sørli, Dag (red.): Lofotboka, årbok for Lofoten.
Sørli, Dag: Øyfolket. Bygdebok for Værøy. bd. 1 og 2. 1976.

Tangstad, Peder: "En gjetergutts oppvekst ved havet", Lofotr, Årbok for Vestvågøy historielag, 1989.
Tekniske meddelelser fra Telegrafstyrelsen, nr.2 1906 (s. 23 -40).
Telegrafverkets historie.
Thesen, Rolv: Lofoten i norsk litteratur og kunst. Aschehoug. 1956.
Thorsvik, Eivind: I storm og stilla. Fiskerihistorie for Nordland. Utgitt av Nordland Fylkes Fiskarlag, Bodø 1982.
Thorsvik, Eivind: Ut mot hav. Fiskerihistorie for Nordland. Utgitt av Nordland Fylkes Fiskarlag. Bodø 1977.
Tørrfisk. Tørrfisknæringens Rek-lamefond, Bergen

Vea, Jan: Motoriseringen av fiskeflåten i Nord-land ca. 1905-1940 med særlig hen-blikk på utviklingen i ytre Vestlofoten. Nord-land Distriktshøgskole 1984.

Wasmuth, Jan: Lofotens fugler. Vestvågøy kommune.
Wold, Helge A.: I paradisets første krets. Cappelen Forlag. 1991.

Ytreberg, N.A.: "Nordlandske Handelssteder". F. Bruns Bokhandels Forlag, Trondheim 1941.

Årbok for Vågan.

OTHER SOURCES
Avskrift fra lydbånd av muntlige informanter i Flakstad og Moskenes.
Ellingsen, Borghild: Foredrag i Bodø radio. (holdt i 1930-åra.)
Folketellingen av år 1900, Moskenes kommune. Riksarkivet.
Kilander, Ingrid: Et år som det passerte i sin almindelighet i mitt hjem, Aa i Lofoten. (skrevet februar 1943.)
Muntlige kilder: Aasmund Sandnes. Petra og Hans Gjertsen.

This is not intended to be a complete Lofoten bibliography.

Unfortunately, it was not possible to provide a translation of Norwegian titles owing to lack of space.

Index

In addition to the Lofoten public museums, there are

Several Other Educational Attractions

· Værøy and Røst

Theme: Isolated villages, living off the land, bird trapping and egg gathering

On the island of Værøy, the isolated and now abandoned hamlet of Måstad is well worth a visit
– a museum in its own right that tells a tale of hard work, moderation and drama, where every natural resource was utilised in the struggle to survive. On the islands of Røst we can still gain some impression of the traditions of egg gathering, bird trapping and sheep herding that were, and still are, of such importance to the people out there in the west.

· The Lofoten Aquarium

8310 Kabelvåg. Tel. 76 07 86 65

Main Theme: Life in the sea

The migration of the cod is, and always has been, the determining factor for the fisheries and settlement in Lofoten. The Aquarium displays fish and life in the sea – from the shoreline to the deep. Slides show.

· Dagmar's Museum of Dolls and Toys

Sakrisøy, 8390 Reine. Tel. 76 09 21 43

Main Theme: "A journey back to childhood" – North Norwegian and European children's culture

"The place that gets to your heart" – small, pleasant museum with exhibition of over 1500 dolls, teddy bears, etc. from 1860-1965. Guided tours.

· The Norwegian Telecommunications Collection

8392 Sørvågen. tel. 76 09 14 88

Main Theme: "Cod and Communications"

A rare museum where exhibitions of telegraphs, wireless telegraphy and wireless telephony provide you with the answer to why Lofoten was to become such an important part of Norwegian and European telecommunications history. Guided tours.

· Lofoten Stockfish Museum

Å i Lofoten. 8392 Sørvågen. Tel. 76 09 12 11

Main Theme: Stockfish – Production and trade

By way of good, systematic exhibitions, guiding and video, thorough information is provided about the landing of fresh fish and the production, sorting, packing and sale of Norway's oldest export commodity, stockfish.

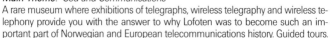

The Public

Museums of Lofoten

exhibitions, demonstrations, activities and sales

· The Lofoten Museum

8310 Kabelvåg. Tel. 76 07 82 23

Main theme: Fishing in Lofoten. The development of stockfish exports in the Middle Ages and Vágar, the fist township in North Norway

Exhibitions and guided tours in an interesting and exciting museum area with:

Prehistoric cultural monuments in Vassosen

"The Medieval Township of Vágar" – archaeological excavation area

Excavations during the summer. Exhibition of finds

Brurberget – one of the country's most important "*Things*", or parliamentary and legislative meeting places

Old squire's residence. Theme exhibitions in the stately mansion dating back to the 1820's: The squire family's everyday life

Collection of Nordland-type boats, including a large *"fembøring"* in the boathouse

The Old Shop – as it was a hundred years ago

Old "rorbu"-environment showing the everyday life of the fishermen

The Lofoten Fishery – theme exhibition (See the "*Footprints in the North*" booklet entitled "*Vágar – the First Town in the North*")

· Vestvågøy Museum

8374 Fygle. Tel. 76 08 00 43

Main Theme 1: The school and municipal administration.

The old school in Fygle was built in 1898.

Exhibitions and guided tours

Reconstruction of one of the old classrooms. Teacher's residence

Rooms used by the council and other boards and committees

In the school yard: outhouse; "rorbu" cabin providing an insight into the everyday life of the fisherman

Main Theme 2: The fisherman-farmer and his family

The fisherman's farm of Skaftnes is situated in idyllic surroundings between Sennesvik and Ure

Farmhouse with interesting and authentic interior

Quayside warehouse with landing station for fish and old shop

Large boathouse with stone walls and collection of Nordland-type boats

Smithy

· Lofotr - The Viking Museum in Borg

8360 Bøstad. Tel. 76 08 49 00

Main Theme: The Iron Age and the chieftain's homestead in Borg as a centre of power during the Viking Age

Impressive reconstruction of the old chieftain's residence in Borg

– as it may have looked around the year 900 AD.

Exhibitions and guided tours of the parts of the building used as banqueting hall, residence and barn

The archaeological excavation sites are an integral part of the museum environment

Exhibition of Viking Age finds from Vestvågøy

Living domestic animals of the old breeds, like wild boar and Nordland horses

Demonstrations of textile work, wood cutting, leather work, bone and horn work, and cooking during the summer. Sale of handicrafts

Transport by horse and carriage to the boathouse down by the fjord. Boat-building and rope-making. Individual activities: rowing the Viking ship "Lofotr" – a replica of the Gokstad ship

Banquets all year round

(See booklet: "*Footprints in the North*" about Lofotr – The Viking Museum in Borg)

· Sund Fisheries Museum

8384 Sund. Tel. 76 09 37 90

Main Theme: *The motorisation of the fishing fleet over the past 100 years*

A small, pleasant museum environment. Guided tours available. Exhibition of boat engines and other technical equipment from the fishing fleet. Several of the engines can be started up. Boathouse with old Nordland-type boats, etc.

"*Curiosity Cabinet*" – collection of old artefacts exhibited in an old "rorbu" cabin

Blacksmith's handicrafts workshop where the smith works in the old-fashioned way

Sale of the popular wrought iron cormorants.

The Old Smith Hans Gjertsen's *Galleri Ambolten* ("Anvil Gallery")

Nearby slipway

· The Norwegian Fishing Village Museum

Å i Lofoten, 8392 Sørvågen. Tel. 76 09 14 88

Main Theme: *Life in the fishing village and the Lofoten Fishery over the past 200 years*

Comprehensive and exciting coastal museum. Educational exhibitions, guided tours, demonstrations, activities and information on video:

The Lofoten Fishery and the tackle and boats used therein. Exhibition in the Main Boathouse – "The World's Greatest Cod Fishery"

Norway's oldest cod-liver oil factory, sale of cod-liver oil – "The long history of cod-liver oil"

Old stockfish production plant, cod heads and roes – "Valuable goods for 1000 years"

The homes of the fisherman's family and the squire – "Social classes"

The "rorbu" cabin and the life of the visiting fisherman – "A hard and perilous life"

The barn and stables – coastal farming north of the Arctic Circle – "Every blade of grass was of value"

Active 150-year old bakery. Sale of fresh baking and local home crafts

Fishing boat trips and sea fishing. Prepare your meal in the authentic Lofoten way

Trips across the Maelstrom to a coastal cave with 3,000 year old cave paintings

(See the "*Footprints in the North*" entitled "*Cave Paintings in Revsvika*")